Other titles include *Up & Running* with:

- *AutoSketch 3*
- *Carbon Copy Plus*
- *Clipper 5.01*
- *dBASE III PLUS*
- *DOS 3.3*
- *DOS 5*
- *DR DOS 5.0*
- *Excel 3 for Windows*
- *Flight Simulator*
- *Grammatik IV 2.0*
- *Harvard Graphics*
- *Harvard Graphics 3*
- *Lotus 1-2-3 Release 2.2*
- *Lotus 1-2-3 for Windows*
- *Lotus 1-2-3 Release 2.3*
- *Lotus 1-2-3 Release 3.1*
- *Mac Classic*
- *Norton Utilities*
- *Norton Utilities 5*
- *Norton Utilities on the Macintosh*
- *PageMaker 4 on the PC*
- *PageMaker on the Macintosh*
- *PC Tools Deluxe 6*
- *PC-Write*
- *PROCOMM PLUS*
- *PROCOMM PLUS 2.0*
- *Q & A*
- *Q & A 4*
- *Quattro Pro 3*
- *Quicken 4*
- *ToolBook for Windows*
- *Turbo Pascal 5.5*
- *Windows 3.0*
- *Windows 286/386*
- *Word for Windows*
- *WordPerfect 5.1*
- *WordPerfect Library/Office PC*
- *XTreeGold 2*
- *Your Hard Disk*

Computer users are not all alike.
Neither are SYBEX books.

We know our customers have a variety of needs. They've told us so. And because we've listened, we've developed several distinct types of books to meet the needs of each of our customers. What are you looking for in computer help?

If you're looking for the basics, try the **ABC's** series, or for a more visual approach, select **Teach Yourself**.

Mastering and **Understanding** titles offer you a step-by-step introduction, plus an in-depth examination of intermediate-level features, to use as you progress.

Our **Up & Running** series is designed for computer-literate consumers who want a no-nonsense overview of new programs. Just 20 basic lessons, and you're on your way.

SYBEX **Encyclopedias** and **Desktop References** provide a comprehensive reference and explanation of all of the commands, features and functions of the subject software.

Sometimes a subject requires a special treatment that our standard series doesn't provide. So you'll find we have titles like **Advanced Techniques, Handbooks, Tips & Tricks**, and others that are specifically tailored to satisfy a unique need.

You'll find SYBEX publishes a variety of books on every popular software package. Looking for computer help? Help Yourself to SYBEX.

For a complete catalog of our publications:

Up & Running with Norton Desktop™ for Windows™

Michael Gross

David J. Clark

San Francisco • Paris • Düsseldorf • Soest

Acquisitions Editor: Dianne King
Series Editor: Joanne Cuthbertson
Editor: Brendan Fletcher
Technical Editor: Sheila Dienes
Word Processors: Ann Dunn, Susan Trybull
Book Designer: Elke Hermanowski
Icon Designer: H. S. Bruno
Screen Graphics: Cuong Le
Desktop Production Artist: H. S. Bruno
Proofreader: Dina F. Quan
Indexer: Ted Laux
Cover Designer: Archer Design

Library of Congress Card Number: 91-65965
ISBN: 0-89588-885-8

Manufactured in the United States of America
10 9 8 7 6 5 4 3 2 1

To our wives, Linda and Janna

SYBEX
Up & Running Books

Who this book is for

The Up & Running series of books from SYBEX has been developed for committed, eager PC users who would like to become familiar with a wide variety of programs and operations as quickly as possible. We assume that you are comfortable with your PC and that you know the basic functions of word processing, spreadsheets, and database management. With this background, Up & Running books will show you in 20 steps what particular products can do and how to use them.

What this book provides

Up & Running books are designed to save you time and money. First, you can avoid purchase mistakes by previewing products before you buy them—exploring their features, strengths, and limitations. Second, once you decide to purchase a product, you can learn its basics quickly by following the 20 steps—even if you are a beginner.

Contents and structure

The first step usually covers software installation in relation to hardware requirements. You'll learn whether the program can operate with your available hardware as well as various methods for starting the program. The second step often introduces the program's user interface. The remaining 18 steps demonstrate the program's basic functions, using examples and short descriptions.

Special symbols and notes

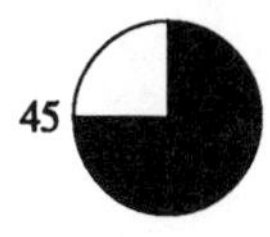

A clock shows the amount of time you can expect to spend at your computer for each step. Naturally, you'll need much less time if you only read through the step rather than complete it at your computer.

You can also focus on particular points by scanning the short notes in the margins and locating the sections you are most interested in.

In addition, three symbols highlight particular sections of text:

The Action symbol highlights important steps that you will carry out.

The Tip symbol indicates a practical hint or special technique.

The Warning symbol alerts you to a potential problem and suggestions for avoiding it.

We have structured the Up & Running books so that the busy user spends little time studying documentation and is not burdened with unnecessary text. An Up & Running book cannot, of course, replace a lengthier book that contains advanced applications. However, you will get the information you need to put the program to practical use and to learn its basic functions in the shortest possible time.

We welcome your comments

SYBEX is very interested in your reactions to the Up & Running series. Your opinions and suggestions will help all of our readers, including yourself. Please send your comments to: SYBEX Editorial Department, 2021 Challenger Drive, Alameda, CA 94501.

Preface

Since its release in 1982, the Norton Utilities package has been the most popular utilities collection on the market. The reason for this is simple: No other software package so efficiently and comprehensively fills the gaps in DOS. With the intoduction of the Norton Destop for Windows, the Peter Norton Group at Symantec Corporation has taken the next logical step and filled some of the gaps in Microsoft Windows' design.

For starters, the Desktop replaces the Windows Program and File Managers with a more streamlined interface. From the Desktop, you can open drive icons simply by clicking on them, much as you would on a Macintosh computer. You can also place icons for programs or files onto the Desktop for easy access.

The Norton Desktop also includes a collection of handy utility programs traditionally associated with the Norton Utilities. You can find lost files with the SuperFind program, recover accidentally deleted data with SmartErase, and examine your hard disk for damage with the Norton Disk Doctor for Windows. In addition, there are several new programs specifically designed for Windows users. The Icon Editor, for example, allows you to edit any of your Windows icons. All of the Desktop's tools—whether based on Norton Utilities programs or designed for Windows—take full advantage of the Windows graphical interface, making them easy to use and understand.

This book will get you "up and running" with the Norton Desktop as quickly as possible. In 20 short steps, you will become familiar with the most important and useful features of the Norton Desktop. When you have completed these steps, you will have a solid grasp of the fundamentals of the Norton Desktop for Windows, and the ability to work more quickly, efficiently, and confidently with Windows.

Table of Contents

Step 1

Installation

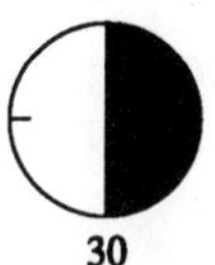

This step guides you through the installation of the Norton Desktop for Windows. It is a straightforward procedure, identical for 5¼" and 3½" disks. Installation should take you about 30 minutes to complete.

Hardware Requirements

In order to run the Norton Desktop, your system must be of the following minimal configuration:

- An IBM AT, 386, 486, PS/2 or 100%-compatible machine.
- DOS 3.1 or later.
- Windows 3.0 or later.
- A hard disk with at least 3.1 megabytes of free space.
- One high-density 5¼" floppy disk drive (1.2Mb) or one 720K 3½" floppy disk drive.
- One megabyte of RAM. Two or more megabytes are recommended.

Though a mouse is not, strictly speaking, necessary for running the program, using one is strongly recommended. This book assumes that you are using a mouse.

Installing the Desktop

During the Norton Desktop installation procedure, there will be on-screen instructions presented in sequential windows. You select options by moving the mouse pointer onto the option you want and clicking the left mouse button, as with other Windows programs.

To begin installation, place Disk 1 in drive A. If Windows is currently running, pull down the Program Manager's File menu and select the Run option. Enter

```
a:install
```

in the resulting window and click OK.

If, however, Windows is not currently running and you are at the DOS prompt, type

```
a:install
```

and press Enter.

Copying the Desktop Files

Registration

Before you copy the program files to your hard disk, you must register the software in your name. You will see a window entitled "Norton Desktop—Registration." Type in your name and company in the appropriate boxes and click OK.

You must type something in the company box, even if it is only a space.

Selecting the desktop directory

Now you should see a window entitled "Install Norton Desktop Files To." The installation program suggests that the Desktop be installed to a directory named \NDW on drive C. If the directory and drive are acceptable and there is sufficient room on your hard disk—the amount of space needed and the amount of space available are indicated by graphs at the bottom of the window—click OK. The install program will begin copying the Desktop files to your hard disk.

If you wish to install the Desktop to a directory other than \NDW or to a drive other than C, type a new path at the Install To prompt, such as

```
d:\ndw
```

or

```
d:\desktop
```

and then click OK. The installation program will copy the Desktop files to your hard disk.

If you do not have enough room to install the Desktop anywhere on your hard disk and you want to install all the Norton applications, you must make room. Cancel installation by clicking on Cancel and following the prompts out of the installation program. Remove files from your hard disk, copying them down to a floppy if necessary, and restart installation.

When prompted to do so, put Disk 2 in drive A and click OK. Repeat this process with the remaining disks. Lastly, you will be prompted to insert the Emergency disk in drive A; do so and click OK.

Modifying Your Computer's Environment

When all of the files have been copied to your hard disk, the installation program will ask to modify your AUTOEXEC.BAT file. You will see the commands that will be inserted into your AUTOEXEC.BAT file in a window. You can have the Norton Desktop installation program insert these lines into your file, save the required changes in a new file, or allow no changes to be made. The default setting allows the Norton Desktop to modify your file. Click OK. This will ensure that necessary features of the Desktop are enabled.

You will next be asked whether you want the Norton Desktop to perform an automatic backup at 4:00 p.m. everyday. Click No. You can establish the automatic backup yourself later with the Scheduler (Step 15) and Backup (Step 8) programs.

You will then be asked if you wish to have the Norton Desktop be your shell for Windows. This makes the Norton Desktop replace the Windows Program Manager. This is the best way to take advantage of the Desktop's capabilities. Click Yes. You will then be notified of the completion of installation. Click OK.

The README.TXT file that now appears in a Notepad window contains last-minute notes that are not included in the documentation. Take a few minutes to read through these notes. When you are finished reading, close the Notepad and exit Windows. Make sure the Save Changes option is selected when you exit.

Reboot your machine. This causes the changes made to your AUTOEXEC.BAT file to take effect. When your machine has rebooted, restart Windows. You are ready to begin working with the Norton Desktop.

Step 2

The Desktop Environment

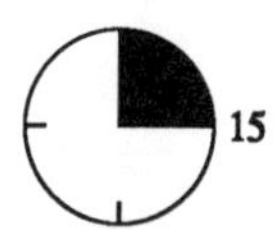

Just as the Norton Utilities have empowered PC users by providing a useful set of tools not found in DOS itself, so the Norton Desktop is designed to make your computer easier to use with Windows. It acts as a sophisticated nerve center for your computer, combining the functions of the Windows Program Manager and File Manager with many functions and capabilities that do not exist in Windows. This step introduces you to the Desktop environment—its appearance, its parts, and its functions. It should take you about 15 minutes to read through this step.

Starting the Desktop

If you have just finished Step 1, Windows, now sporting the Norton Desktop in place of the Program Manager, should be running on your computer. If it is not, please start it. Close any open windows you see by double-clicking on their control bars or selecting Close from the Control menu. Your screen should look something like Figure 2.1.

Desktop Mechanics

Using pull-down menus

At a very basic, mechanical level, Windows with the Norton Desktop and Windows without the Desktop are quite similar. You will find pull-down menus at the top of the Norton Desktop screen, just as you would at the top of the Program Manager screen. The menus here work just like the menus in the Program Manager or any other Windows application. If you wish to satisfy yourself on this point, click on File on the menu bar to pull down the File menu and then click outside of the menu to close it up again.

Under the Norton Desktop, icons and windows also work just as they work under the Program Manager: To move an icon you drag it with the mouse; double-clicking on an icon starts the program associated with it. To move a window, you drag it with the mouse by its title bar. You resize a window by dragging its borders.

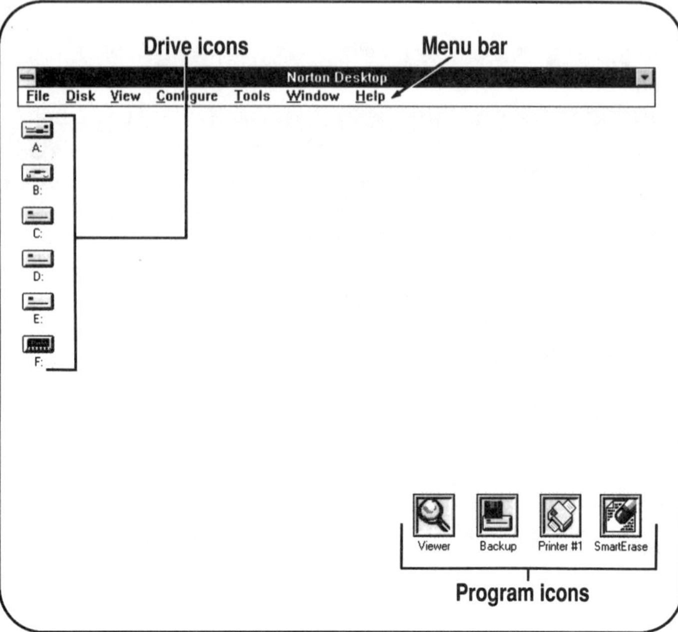

Figure 2.1: The Norton Desktop

Parts of the Desktop

Beyond these similarities, however, running Windows with the Norton Desktop is rather different from running Windows without it.

The Drive Icons

Desktop file functions

Along the upper left side of the screen is a column of icons representing each of the drives installed on your system. These icons give you access to file functions such as copying, moving, and deleting. Under Windows, these functions are inconveniently located within the Windows File Manager. Here they are right on the Desktop, where they are easier to get at and use.

If you want to experiment with a drive icon, double-click on the C icon. You will see a window similar to those you have seen in the Windows File Manager, with the directory tree displayed in the left portion of the window and the file list on the right. Close this window when you've finished looking.

The drive icons also give you access to several file functions that are not available from within the Windows File Manager. You can view the contents of most kinds of files—not only text files, but spreadsheet, database, binary, archive, and graphics files as well—directly from the Desktop. You can also use the Desktop to search for text within files.

File functions will be discussed in more detail in Steps 4 and 5.

The Program Icons

Programs on the Desktop

In the lower right portion of your screen you should see a row of four program icons. These four icons look like any other four minimized icons you might see when running Windows with just the Program Manager; however, the programs represented by these icons are not running. Minimized programs under the Windows Program Manager are running, at least in the background. With the Norton Desktop, it is possible to put program icons on the Desktop without running the program first. That is, you can take individual icons out of their groups and put them on the Desktop. This makes it much easier to access your most frequently used programs.

Just as the Desktop gives you more program icon flexibility, so too does it enhance the flexibility of your program groups (though no groups are visible on your screen at the moment; the windows you closed earlier were groups). As with the Program Manager, you can organize your icons into separate group windows, opening and minimizing the groups as the need arises. You can also place group windows anywhere on the screen (not just within the Program Manager window); and you can nest groups (that is, you can make groups within groups if your organizational scheme calls for this).

Working with groups will be discussed in greater detail in Step 3.

Norton Desktop Menus

The Norton Desktop could justifiably be called "The Norton Utilities for Windows," as it provides far more than an improved Program Manager and File Manager. The package comes with its own set of utility programs, some of which will be familiar to users of the Norton Utilities. Others are new, but all can be run from the Desktop pull-down menus. These menus are described below.

- File: Contains functions for basic file maintenance—Copy, Move, Delete, and others.
- Disk: Contains basic disk functions. From this menu you can copy, label, and format a disk.
- View: Contains functions for adjusting "file manager" windows and for viewing the contents of files.
- Configure: Contains functions for customizing the Desktop.
- Tools: This is the menu from which each of the Desktop utility programs can be run.
- Window: Provides commands that govern the way windows display information on the Desktop. The Window menu also displays all existing program groups and allows you to open them. Groups are discussed in more detail in Step 3.
- Help: Provides online information organized in several different ways—Index, Keyboard, Commands, Procedures, and Using Help.

By default, the Desktop's menu's are abbreviated, or "short," and so all of these options are not visible. To use the "full" menus, pull down the Configure menu and select the Full Menus option. The remainder of this book assumes that full menus are enabled.

If you wish to do so, you can exit Windows now by pulling down the File menu and selecting Exit. Otherwise, let's move on to Step 3.

Step 3

Quick Access

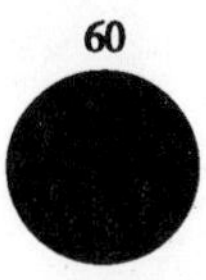

Quick Access is the Norton Desktop's answer to the Windows Program Manager. Like the Program Manager, Quick Access is composed of group windows and icons, and it is used to organize and run programs. Quick Access is, however, more flexible and capable than its Windows counterpart. Group windows are not confined within a window, as they are in the Program Manager, but can be moved freely around the screen. They can also be nested inside one another. Icons can represent both programs and individual data files.

In this step, you will put Quick Access through its paces. The tutorial should take you about one hour to complete.

Creating and Manipulating Group Windows

Using program groups

Typically in Windows, groups are used to arrange your computer's programs into groups of related tasks. They appear as numbered menu items on the Window menu of the Program Manager. For instance, the Games group that was formed automatically when you installed Windows contains two programs, Solitaire and Reversi—both games. When you want to play a game, you pull down the Window menu from the Program Manager and select the Games group. The Games window opens and you can click on the desired icon to start the program.

Norton Quick Access windows improve on this capability, as we shall see in the following section.

Let's jump right in and begin.

1. If Windows is not running, please start it.
2. Pull down the Window menu and select Quick Access. This brings up the Quick Access window, which will look much like the one shown in Figure 3.1.

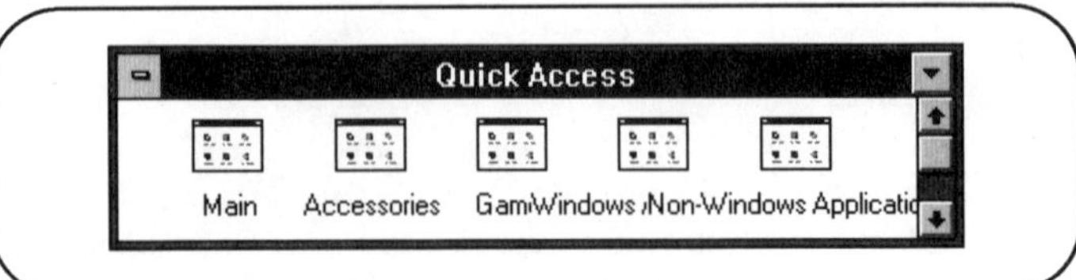

Figure 3.1: The Norton Quick Access window

Notice that the Quick Access window is similar in configuration to the Program Manager: The Quick Access group icons even have the same names as the Program Manager's groups. This is because the Desktop uses the Program Manager as a model when it builds the Quick Access groups. In the next four sections, you will work through the ins and outs of Quick Access groups.

Basic Group Manipulation

In this section you will explore opening, closing, and moving groups.

1. Open a group window by double-clicking on its icon.
2. Now move the window by dragging it by its title bar to another location on the screen.
3. Close the Norton Quick Access window by double-clicking on the control box or selecting Close on the Control menu. Close the group you opened in step 1.
4. Pull down the Window menu and select any group listed. The group selected will open alone.
5. Close the group window and reopen the Norton Quick Access window.

Notice that a group window is not a document window; it is not confined within another window. In fact, you can use group windows independently of one another.

List View

Programs within any group can be represented as icons or in a list.

1. Pull down the Window menu and select the View As option.
2. In the View Group As box on the dialog window that appears, select the List option and click OK. The contents of the Quick Access window change from a collection of icons to a list, as shown in Figure 3.2.

To change all groups to List view, toggle on the Change All Groups option in the dialog window discussed in step 2 above. When this option is off, only the current or active group changes views.

Repeat the steps above to change the view back to Icon view, as the rest of the tutorial assumes that you are not in List view.

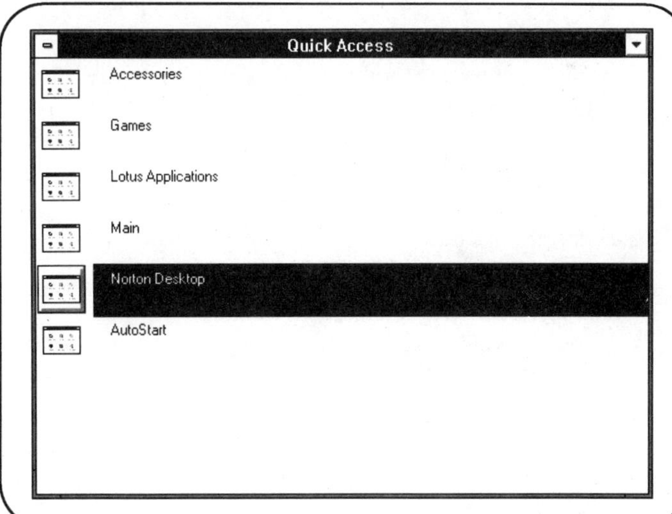

Figure 3.2: List view

Creating New Groups

You should use groups to organize your work in the way that best suits you. Your organizational scheme will probably require groups other than the default groups you have at the moment. To create a new group, follow these steps:

1. If the Quick Access window is no longer open, open it now by selecting Quick Access from the Window menu.
2. Pull down the File menu and select the New option. This brings up the New dialog window shown in Figure 3.3.
3. In the Type box, select the Group option if it is not already selected.
4. Click the box beneath the Title prompt and type

   `Group 3.1`

   This is the name of the group that will appear as the label under the group icon or as the title of the group window.
5. You may want to click in the box under the Description prompt to enter a description of the group's intended use. For example, enter

   `This is the first sample group used in Step 3.`

   as this group's description.
6. Click OK and the new empty group window will appear, ready to fill with programs, data files, or other groups. Close this window for now. The new group will appear as an icon in the Quick Access window.

Nesting Groups

It may make sense in your organizational scheme to put certain groups within others. For example, you could create a group for your letters and a group for your memos, and then put both the letters group and the memos group within a corrspondence group.

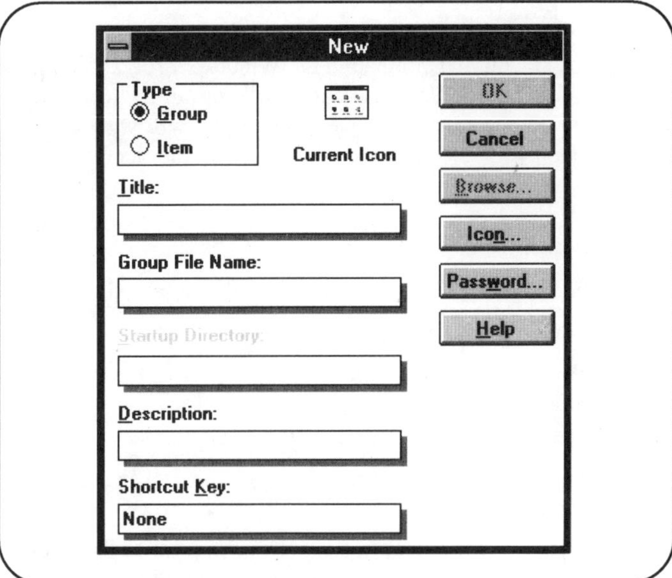

Figure 3.3: The New dialog window

Quick Access makes this process, also known as *nesting* groups, easy.

1. Repeat the steps in the section above to create another group. Call this one Group 3.2.
2. Drag the first sample group icon, Group 3.1, into the second group's window.
3. Close Group 3.2. Notice that Group 3.1 is nowhere to be seen. You have nested the groups.

Icons

In Quick Access, icons can represent two kinds of files, program files and data files. For example, you can have an icon representing your word processor and an icon representing each document you create with that word processor. In the next three sections, you will use icons in both of these capacities.

Program Icons

Any program icon that you had in the Windows Program Manager when you first ran the Norton Desktop will appear in Quick Access. There may be occasions, however, where you will want to add a program icon yourself. Here we will create another icon to run the Windows Notepad.

1. Reopen Group 3.2.
2. Pull down the File menu and select the New option again.
3. In the Type box, select the Item option.
4. In the box under the Title prompt, type

   `Notepad II`

   This will be the title of the program icon you are now creating.
5. In the box under the Program/Document/Script prompt, type

   `notepad.exe`

   This is the complete file name of the program you want the icon to represent. Do not enter a path here. That is done in the next step.
6. In the box under the Startup Directory prompt, type

   `c:\windows`

   This is the directory that contains the file you specified in step 5.
7. In the box under the Description prompt, you can enter a description of this icon if you wish.
8. Click on the box under the Shortcut Key prompt. Here you can enter a Ctrl-key combination. Pressing this key combination will start the program as if you had double-clicked on the icon. Press Ctrl-N, for Notepad. You should see "Ctrl+N" appear in the box.

9. Click OK. The Notepad II icon should appear inside the Group 3.2 window alongside the Group 3.1 icon.
10. Press Ctrl-N or double-click on the icon to start the Notepad.
11. Close the Notepad again.

Associating Files

Using file extensions to associate files

Icons can represent either programs or data files. When an icon represents a data file, double-clicking on it will start the program you used to create the data file and the program will have that file loaded. This can be quite useful for accessing your commonly used files. Before such an arrangement will work, however, data files must be properly associated with the programs used to create them. To associate files, you match program names with file extensions. Follow these steps to associate sample .SMP files with the Windows Notepad:

1. Pull down the File menu and select the Associate option. This will bring up an Associate dialog window like the one shown in Figure 3.4.
2. Click on Add.
3. At the Program prompt, type the file name of the program:

   `notepad.exe`

4. At the Extension prompt, type the extension you want to associate with the program you typed in the previous step.

   `smp`

   Make sure you do not type a period before the extension.
5. Click OK. The association will appear in the list of associations.
6. Click OK again.

If you wish to change an association that already exists, follow the steps above, but click Edit instead of Add in the second step.

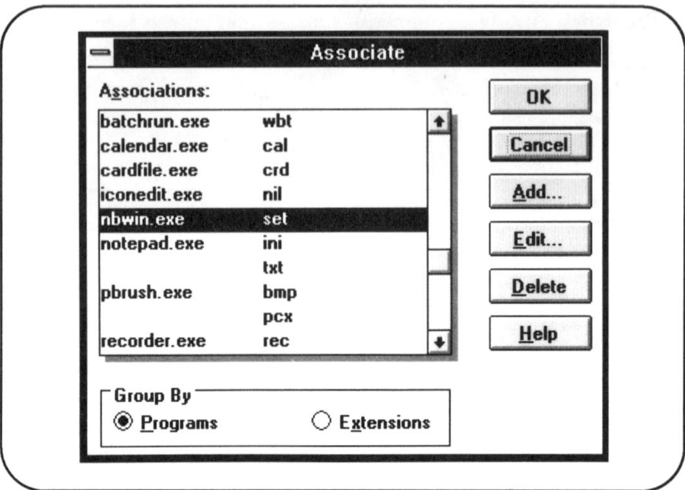

Figure 3.4: The Associate dialog window

Data Icons

Now that an association exists, we will create a sample Notepad file and a data icon representing that file.

1. Start the Notepad again.
2. Type

   `This is the sample data file used in Step 3.`

3. Pull down the File menu and select the Save As option. Save the file under the name C:\NDW\STEP3FIL.SMP.
4. Close the Notepad.
5. Follow the steps for creating a new icon listed in the "Program Icons" section above, but fill in the blanks as listed in Table 3.1.

Prompt	*Entry*
Title:	None. Filename supplied automatically
Program/Document/Script:	STEP3FIL.SMP
Startup Directory:	C:\NDW
Description:	none
Shortcut Key:	none

Table 3.1: Creating a Data Icon

When you have finished, a new icon will appear in the Group 3.1 window. Double-click on the icon. The Notepad will start with the sample file loaded. When you've finished examining the sample file, close the Notepad.

AutoStart

Quick Access gives you the unique ability to remove icons from their groups and put them right out on the Desktop. From the Desktop, you need only double-click the appropriate icons to access your commonly used programs or files. You can also place group icons on the Desktop. Try this now by dragging some of the icons from the Group 3.2 window onto the Desktop and back into the Group 3.2 window.

When you put an icon on the Desktop, it will stay there until you close it by clicking it once and selecting Close. If you quit the Desktop and restart it, any icon you put out on the Desktop will be there. This is convenient if there are programs or files that you use all the time that you want on the Desktop. You don't want to have to drag them out each time you start up in the morning.

Suppose, however, you want to launch a specific program (like your word processor or spreadsheet) or open a specific data file automatically every time you start Windows. The Norton Desktop provides a simple and convenient way to do this called AutoStart. To learn how to launch an application automatically when you start Windows, follow the steps below:

1. Pull down the Configure menu and select the Preferences option.
2. Toggle on the Save Configuration on Exit option, if it is not on already, and click OK.

Preserving changes to your groups

These two steps are equivalent to the Save Changes option you encounter when exiting Windows when using it without the Norton Desktop. Toggling on this option ensures that changes in your groups are preserved from session to session. Having toggled it on now (if it was off), you do not have to repeat these steps again.

3. Open the AutoStart window by pulling down the Window menu and selecting AutoStart.
4. Drag the Notepad II icon from the Group 3.2 window into the AutoStart window.
5. Quit the Desktop by pulling down the File menu and selecting the Exit option.
6. Restart Windows. The Notepad will open a new active window.
7. Close the Notepad.

Deleting Groups and Icons

This brings you to the end of the tutorial and the end of the step. You may wish to discard the sample groups or icons created here. Make sure to delete Notepad II from the AutoStart window (unless you want Notepad II to start automatically each time you run Windows). Follow these steps to delete a group or icon:

1. Click once on the icon or group to be removed. Note that groups can only be deleted when represented as an icon.
2. Pull down the File menu and select the Delete option.
3. Click Yes when asked for confirmation of the deletion.

Step 4

Basic File Functions

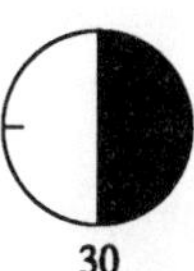

Housekeeping (otherwise known as file management) is a necessary part of using a computer. Let it go for too long and soon you will have a proliferation of unorganized and probably unnecessary files on your hard disk. This makes finding the files you do want that much more difficult. This step contains a tutorial on performing basic file functions with the Norton Desktop—making directories and copying, moving, and deleting files. It should take you about 30 minutes to complete.

Drive Icons and Drive Windows

The Norton Desktop's file functions are located in a column of drive icons on the upper left portion of the screen. Begin the tutorial by double-clicking on the C drive icon. This opens a drive window like the one shown in Figure 4.1. The left panel shows the directory tree for the current drive (C:) and the right panel shows the contents of the currently selected directory. It is on this window and others like it that file functions are actually carried out.

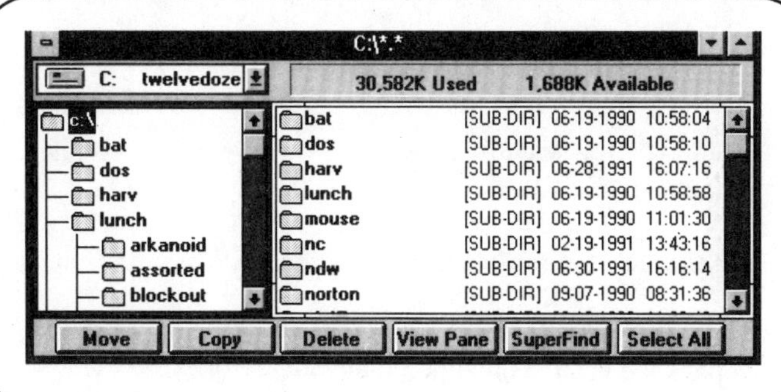

Figure 4.1: The C drive window

Creating Sample Directories and Files

Creating sample directories

In the exercises that follow, we will need to delete some files, so rather than working with any of your existing files or directories, we will create new ones. Follow these steps to create two sample directories:

1. If the title bar of your drive window does not read "C:*.*," then you need to get to the root directory of the C drive. Scroll to the top of the directory tree panel and click once on the root directory icon labeled "C:\." This ensures that the sample directories you make will be subdirectories of the root directory.
2. With Full Menus enabled, pull down the File menu and select the Make Directory option.
3. On the dialog window that appears, type

   `sample`

   and then click OK. This creates the sample directory C:\SAMPLE.
4. Pull down the File menu again and select the Make Directory option.
5. This time enter

   `scratch`

   on the dialog window and click OK to create the sample directory C:\SCRATCH.

Creating sample files

Now make three short sample text files using the Windows Notepad.

1. Pull down the Window menu and select Accessories. This opens the group containing the Notepad icon.
2. Double-click on the Notepad icon to start the program.
3. Type a little sample text, garbage if you want.

4. Using the Save As option on the File menu, save the first file under the name

   `c:\sample\step4a`

5. Again using the Save As option, save the second file under the name

   `c:\sample\step4b`

   and the third under the name

   `c:\sample\step4c`

6. Close the Notepad and the Accessories group.

Checking your work

Scroll the directory tree down until the SAMPLE and SCRATCH directories are visible, if they are not visible already. Click once on the SAMPLE folder and the three sample files will appear in the file list panel.

Copying Files

Copy is probably the file function you will use most frequently. In this portion of the tutorial, you will copy your three sample files—first one and then the other two together—to the SCRATCH directory.

Copying One File

Copying a single file is a simple operation.

1. Highlight the file STEP4A.TXT by clicking on its name in the file list panel.
2. On the row of buttons at the bottom of the C drive window, click Copy. If you prefer using pull-down menus, you can pull down the File menu and select the Copy option instead.

3. A dialog window prompts you for the name of the directory to which you want to copy the file. Type

   ```
   c:\scratch
   ```

   and click OK. That's all there is to it.

It is also possible to copy a file by dragging its icon from the file list to its target directory on the directory tree. Try this now by clicking on the STEP4A.TXT icon and dragging it to the SCRATCH directory folder. On the warning window that asks if you wish to overwrite the file, click No.

Copying Multiple Files

If you have a number of files to copy to the same directory, repeating the above steps for each file individually would be terribly inefficient. Copying two or more files simultaneously is a simple variation on the above operation.

1. Highlight the files STEP4B.TXT and STEP4C.TXT. Click once on STEP4B.TXT and then, while holding down the Ctrl key, click once on STEP4C.TXT.
2. Click on the Copy button again.
3. The target directory, C:\SCRATCH, will already be selected from the last copy operation. Click OK to copy these files to the C:\SCRATCH directory.
4. Now click on the SCRATCH folder on the directory tree to see the list of files in that directory. The three sample files should appear in the file list panel.

You can also copy multiple files by dragging them. First highlight all of the files you wish to copy and then drag their icons to the target directory folder.

Deleting Files

Files can also be deleted one at a time or in groups. Follow these steps to delete the copies of the sample files in the SCRATCH directory.

1. Highlight all of the files by holding down the Ctrl key and clicking on the file names in the file list panel.
2. On the row of buttons at the bottom of the C drive window, click Delete. If you prefer using pull-down menus, you'll find the Delete function on the File pull-down menu.
3. Click OK on the Delete dialog window.
4. A warning dialog window will appear asking if you want to delete the first file, STEP4.TXT. Clicking Yes would delete that file but you will still be warned about each file in turn. Click Yes To All to delete the entire list. The sample files should now be gone from the SCRATCH directory file list.

Moving Files

Occasionally you'll find it more convenient to move files instead of copying them. The Copy command leaves you with two copies of a file—the original and a copy at another location on disk. The Move command leaves you with one. It effectively copies the files and deletes the originals in one operation. To conclude the tutorial, return to the SAMPLE directory and move the three sample files to the SCRATCH directory.

1. To return to the SAMPLE directory, click on the SAMPLE folder on the directory tree. The three sample files should appear in the file list.
2. Highlight all three files on the file list. (Hold down the Ctrl key and click on each of their names in turn.)
3. On the row of buttons at the bottom of the window, click the Move button.

4. On the dialog window that appears, C:\SCRATCH will again appear from the previous Copy operation. Click OK. The files should disappear from the file list panel.
5. Click on the SCRATCH folder on the directory tree to see that the files arrived in the SCRATCH directory as intended.

Delete the files from the SCRATCH directory using the instructions from the preceding section. They will no longer be needed. Keep the two sample directories, however, as they will be used in Step 5.

Step 5

Finding and Viewing Files

30

With the recent proliferation of large hard disks, it has become quite easy to lose files among the hundreds, if not thousands, of files you can easily keep. As hard disks grow larger, the ability to find misplaced files becomes more valuable. Viewing files is also a valuable capability, as it allows you to see what a file contains without starting up the application it was created with. This step introduces you to the Norton Desktop's file-finding and file-viewing functions. The tutorial covering these functions should take you about 30 minutes to complete.

In addition to the tutorial, this step contains a summary discussion of the file functions that have not been treated here or in Step 4.

Creating Sample Files

Before the tutorial actually begins, use the Windows Notepad to create two sample files to find and view. In the first, type

```
This is the first sample file used in Step 5.
```

and save it under the name C:\SAMPLE\STEP5A.TXT. In the second, type

```
This is the second sample file used in Step 5.
```

and save it under the name C:\SCRATCH\STEP5B.TXT. Make sure to include the path along with each file name. This will ensure that the files are "lost" in a few different directories. Close the Notepad and Accessories window when you are done.

Finding Files

Norton SuperFind

Now that your sample files are conveniently lost, begin the tutorial by "finding" them again.

1. Open the C drive window, if it isn't already open, by double-clicking on the C drive icon.
2. Click the SuperFind button. Alternatively, you can pull down the Tools menu and select the SuperFind option. The SuperFind window shown in Figure 5.1 appears.
3. At the Find Files prompt, type

   `step5*.*`

   This tells the file finder to look for every file name beginning with the characters S-T-E-P-5.
4. At the Where prompt, you can specify the area of your disk or disks to be searched. Click on the downward-pointing arrow to display the list of available options, then click on the desired item in the list. The default option, (Current Drive only), is sufficient for the tutorial and will almost always be the option you use if you have only one hard disk. If you have more than one, you should use the (All Drives) or (All Drives Except Floppies) options.
5. Click Find. SuperFind will list the files it finds in a window such as that shown in Figure 5.2. (You should see the two sample files and any others you might have beginning with the characters S-T-E-P-5.) SuperFind displays not only a file's name but also its essential characteristics and, most importantly, the directory in which it is located.
6. Now close the window listing the results of your file search by clicking on its control box.

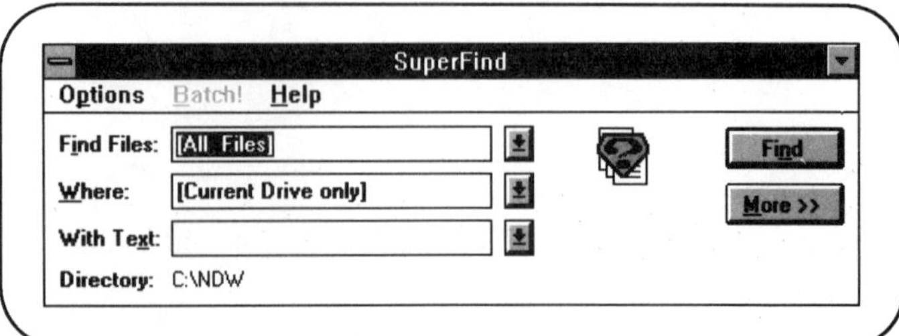

Figure 5.1: The Norton SuperFind window

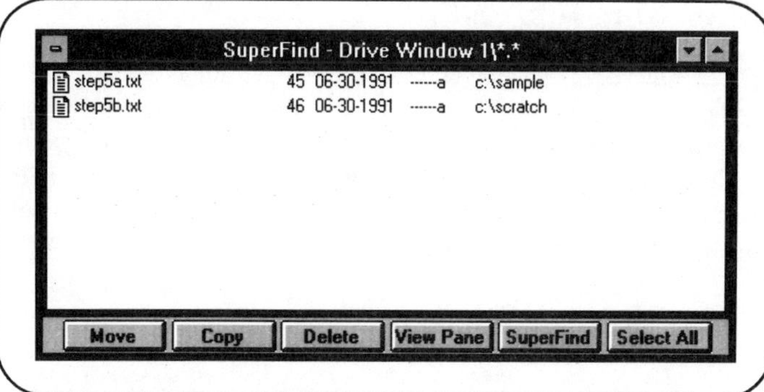

Figure 5.2: The results of a file find

The Find Files prompt has a drop-down list that gives you the option of searching for files by type or extension. To see this list, click on the downward-pointing arrow. If you know the file extension of the file you're looking for, you can narrow down your search by selecting the appropriate option. To see, add to, or edit the search criteria for each of these file classes, pull down the SuperFind Options menu and select Search Sets. Table 5.1 lists these sets, the file extensions they search for, and some of the programs that create such files.

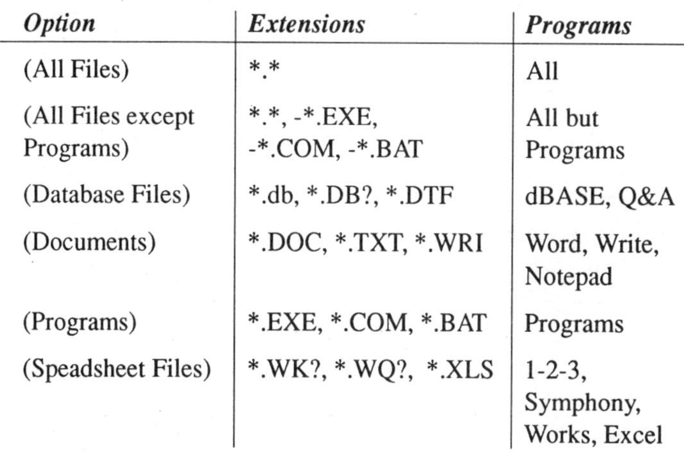

Option	*Extensions*	*Programs*
(All Files)	*.*	All
(All Files except Programs)	*.*, -*.EXE, -*.COM, -*.BAT	All but Programs
(Database Files)	*.db, *.DB?, *.DTF	dBASE, Q&A
(Documents)	*.DOC, *.TXT, *.WRI	Word, Write, Notepad
(Programs)	*.EXE, *.COM, *.BAT	Programs
(Speadsheet Files)	*.WK?, *.WQ?, *.XLS	1-2-3, Symphony, Works, Excel

Table 5.1: SuperFind search sets

Searching for Text

There may be times when you can't remember the name of a file but you do know what is in it. Perhaps someone else created the file or perhaps its name just slipped your mind. You will not be able to find a file using the search detailed above if you don't know its name. Fortunately, you can search for a file by looking for a particular string of text that you know is in it.

To search for a text string, do the following:

1. Pull down the Tools menu and select the SuperFind option as before. Notice the With Text prompt.
2. Drop down the list next to Find Files and select the (Documents) option, since you know you will be looking for a file created with the Windows Notepad. You could leave the setting at the (All Files) option, but searching through all file types takes longer than just searching through document files. It is to your advantage, then, to narrow the search as much as you can by looking through a particular kind of file rather than through all files.
3. Keep the setting at (Current Drive only) at the Where prompt. You will want to use this option unless you have more than one hard disk, in which case you should use the (All Drives Except Floppies) option.
4. At the With Text prompt, type

   ```
   This is the second
   ```

   and then click Find.
5. The search finds the second sample file STEP5B.TXT, and any other document file that happens to contain the text specified above. Now close the Norton SuperFind window.

Viewing Files

The Norton Viewer

Often you will want to know just what a particular file is or contains. The Viewer allows you to do this without opening the application used to create the file. The Viewer is particularly helpful if you don't know what that application is. Let's use the Viewer to look at the contents of one of the sample files.

1. Click on the SAMPLE folder.
2. Highlight the STEP5A.TXT file by clicking once on it.
3. Click the View Pane button. This starts the Norton Viewer, which will display the contents of this sample file in a new pane within the drive window. Click View Pane once more to close the View Pane.
4. Now highlight STEP5A.TXT again and drag its icon onto the Viewer icon displayed in the Desktop. This brings up a full-screen version of the Viewer. (You can also accomplish this by selecting View from the File menu if you prefer.)

The Viewer can display the contents of text files, spreadsheet files, database, files, graphics files, binary (program) files, and archive files. It knows which is which by looking at a file's extension. If, however, you try to view an extensionless file, or one with an extension the Viewer doesn't recognize, you may not at first be able to see the contents of your file. To remedy this situation, pull down the Viewer's Viewer menu and select the Set Current Viewer option. On the dialog window that appears, select the kind of file you are viewing from the list and click OK. Your file should then be visible.

Close the Viewer and the C drive window by double-clicking on their control boxes.

Other File Functions

There are some other file functions not discussed in this tutorial or in the previous step. All are available on the Desktop's File menu. These are listed below.

File options

- Run: Runs a Windows or non-Windows program. You can also run a program by double-clicking on it in a drive window.

- Run DOS: Temporarily exits or "shells out" to the DOS prompt.
- Print: Prints a text file. You can also run this from the Printer icon on the Desktop or by dropping a file's icon on the printer icon.
- Edit: Opens a text file for editing. The default editor is the Windows Notepad. This can be changed from the Configure/Editor option.
- Rename: Renames a file or directory
- Properties: When applied to file, sets or clears file attributes. Files can have one of four properties or attributes. These are as follows:
    - System: Makes a disk bootable and applies only to the DOS system files.
    - Hidden: Causes a file not to be displayed in a directory listing.
    - Read-Only: Write-protects a file.
    - Archive: Allows files to be backed up with the DOS BACKUP program.

When applied to an icon, Properties allows you to replace the icon with another or change its title.

Step 6

Unerasing Files

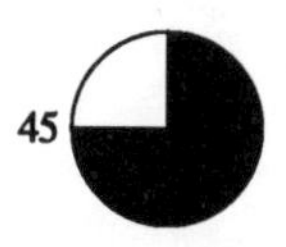

Every computer user has, at one time or another, unintentionally deleted an important file or had it done to him or her. The ability to recover or "unerase" deleted files is the feature that made the Norton Utilities famous. The Norton Desktop has this ability as well.

Unerasing a deleted file is possible because of the way DOS organizes your disks. When you delete a file, DOS considers the space the file occupied to be available for use again, and it will eventually write a new file or files onto that space. The data contained in the erased file is not destroyed, however; it remains on the disk. The erased file, then, can be recovered as long as no new files have been written over its data.

The TRASHCAN directory

To prevent erased files from being overwritten, the Desktop stores the data of deleted files in a special hidden directory called TRASHCAN. When it comes time to recover a file, successful unerasure is virtually guaranteed as its data can simply be reclaimed from TRASHCAN.

This step contains a tutorial on unerasing files with the Desktop's SmartErase tool. You will create a short text file, delete it, and then unerase it. This step also contains a section on configuring and manipulating TRASHCAN. It should take you about 45 minutes to work through this step.

Making and Deleting a Sample File

The Erase Protect program

Before you begin the tutorial, indeed, before you use SmartErase regularly, the Erase Protect (EP) program must be loaded. Erase Protect is the program that SmartErase actually uses to move files into TRASHCAN, though the user has no contact with it once it is installed. If you followed the installation instructions in Step 1, Erase Protect should already be loaded. If you chose not to install Erase Protect during main installation, put the following line in your AUTOEXEC.BAT file:

```
EP /ON
```

Then reboot your system and restart Windows.

Once you have made sure that EP is in place, follow these steps to create and erase your sample file:

1. Open the Windows Notepad again and type the following text at a blank or new screen:

   This file will be used to test the SmartErase tool. It will be created, deleted, and unerased.

2. Save the file as C:\SCRATCH\UNERASE.ME!. This will put the file in the SCRATCH directory that you created back in Step 4.
3. Once you have saved the file, close any open windows.
4. Open the C drive window and click once on the SCRATCH directory icon to change to the SCRATCH directory. The sample file should appear in the file list.
5. Highlight the sample file and delete it, then close the C drive window.

Unerasing Files

Unerasing files with the Desktop is a largely automated procedure closely resembling the basic file functions you learned in Step 4. To unerase the sample file, follow these steps:

1. Start SmartErase by double-clicking on the SmartErase icon, or pull down the Tools menu and select the UnErase option. This brings up the SmartErase window shown in Figure 6.1. Notice that it is quite similar to the drive windows, with a directory tree in the left panel and a file list in the right. In this case, though, the file list is a list of erased

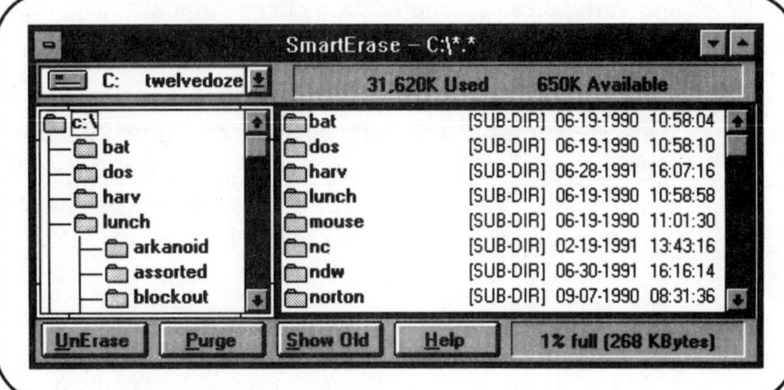

Figure 6.1: The SmartErase window

files, not current files. Directories listed here, however, are the directories currently on your disk.

2. Change to the SCRATCH directory by clicking on the SCRATCH directory icon. The erased sample file should appear in the file list, along with any other files that have previously been erased from this directory.

3. Now highlight the sample file, UNERASE.ME!, by clicking on it once.
4. Click the UnErase button to unerase the file.

The sample file is now recovered and it should disappear from the SmartErase file list.

It is possible to unerase files that were deleted when Erase Protect was not on, though successful recovery is less likely than if Erase Protect was on. The procedure differs only slightly from that outlined above. For these files, you will be asked to supply the first letter of the file name, which was lost when the file was erased.

Checking the Recovered File

The unerased sample file is as good as new, as if it had never been deleted in the first place. Let's check it, just to make sure.

1. Reopen the drive C window and change again to the SCRATCH directory, if necessary. UNERASE.ME! should be visible in the file list.
2. View the contents of the sample file by dragging its icon onto the Viewer icon. You should see the text you typed earlier. (If necessary, pull down the View menu and select the Change option to tell the Viewer it is showing a text file.)
3. Close all open windows.

Configuring SmartErase

As mentioned in the introduction to this step, the Desktop more or less assures successful unerasure by moving erased data into a protected directory called TRASHCAN. By default, all files that are erased from your hard disk are moved into TRASHCAN. They will remain there for five days before they are automatically removed, or "purged." When configuring SmartErase, you can specify the size of TRASHCAN, which erased files are moved into it, and how long they stay there before being purged. To configure SmartErase, follow these steps:

1. Pull down the Configure menu and select the SmartErase option. This brings up the dialog window shown in Figure 6.2.
2. In the Drives to Protect box, all drives on your system appear and your hard disk should be highlighted. Only files from drives highlighted here are moved into TRASHCAN when erased. In general, it is not necessary to protect floppy drives, though if you work on a "public" machine and do not store data on its hard disk, you might want to do so. Click once to highlight (or unhighlight) a drive.
3. In the Files to Protect box, you can specify which files are moved into TRASHCAN when erased. By default, all files (*.*) are protected. Other file protection options are listed

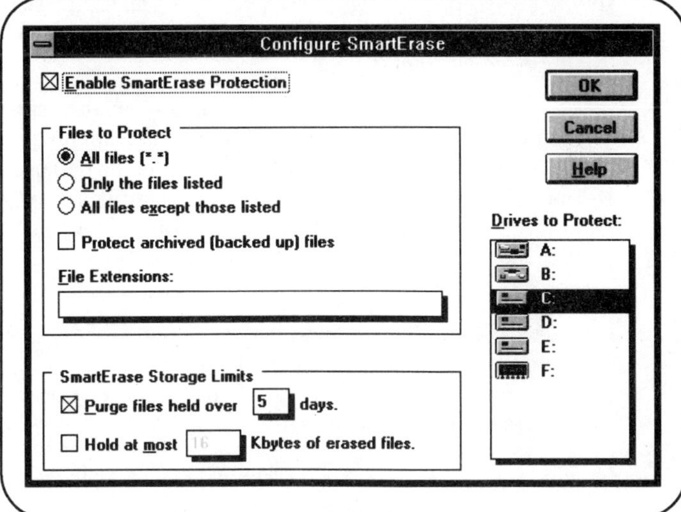

Figure 6.2: Configuring SmartErase

as follows:

- Only the files listed: Only files listed at the File Extensions prompt will be put into the TRASHCAN when erased. Files must be listed by extension or type. You should use this option to specify all program files (*.COM, *.EXE, *.BAT) and data files (*.DOC, *.DBF, *.WK1, etc.). This prevents TRASHCAN from being filled up with unnecessary files such as temporary files created by programs, which are sometimes quite large.
- All files except those listed: Protects all files other than the ones you specify at the File Extensions prompt. Again, files should be specified by extension or type.
- Protect archived (backed up) files: If you regularly use a backup program to back up your files, you may not need to unerase them if they are deleted. You can just copy them back onto your hard disk. If you do not want such backed up files placed in TRASHCAN when they are deleted, leave this option off.

4. In the SmartErase Storage Limits box, you can set the size of the TRASHCAN and the amount of time files are held there before they are purged.
   - Toggle on the Purge files held over option and then enter the number of days files are held before they are removed from TRASHCAN. For normal use, the default is fine. Those who traffic in many hundreds of files weekly, or those who keep particularly critical information on their computers, might consider extending this a bit.

   - Toggle on the Hold at most option to set the size of TRASHCAN. Keep in mind that the larger TRASHCAN is, the less room you have on you hard disk for active files. However, if TRASHCAN is full, a newly erased file will not be put into it.
5. When you have set all the options the way you want them, click OK.

Purging Files Manually

Occasionally it will become necessary to remove a file from TRASHCAN yourself, rather than waiting for an automatic purge—when TRASHCAN fills up, for example. Keep in mind, however, that if you remove a file from TRASHCAN, it will not be possible to unerase it. This sequence of steps, similar to the sequence for copying, moving, or unerasing files, will conclude this step.

1. Start SmartErase by double-clicking on the SmartErase icon, or pull down the Tools menu and select the UnErase option.
2. Highlight the file or files you wish to remove from TRASHCAN, clicking relevant directories first, if necessary.
3. Click the Purge button.
4. When asked if you wish to permanently remove the highlighted files, click Yes.

Running UnErase from the Emergency Disk

If you do all your work within Windows, the procedures outlined in this step are sufficient to recover any file you accidentally deleted while working in Windows. If you should accidentally erase a file while working at the DOS prompt when Windows is not loaded, do not start Windows to unerase these files! Doing so may overwrite that data you intend to unerase (particularly if Erase Protect is not loaded). To unerase files deleted under these circumstances, follow these steps:

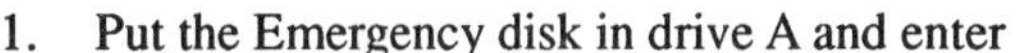

1. Put the Emergency disk in drive A and enter

   ```
   a:unerase
   ```

2. If the file you want does not appear on the file list on the screen, it is probably in another directory. Pull down the File menu and select the change diRectory option. Then, on the directory tree that appears, highlight the directory you want and click OK.
3. Highlight the file you want to unerase by clicking once on its name.
4. Select the UnErase option to recover the file.
5. Since the first letter of the file name was lost when the file was erased, press a letter to restore it. The file, once unerased, will start with the letter you type.

You may unerase any number of other files by repeating the above procedure. When you are done, select Quit! from the menu bar at the top of the screen to exit the program and return to the DOS prompt.

Step 7

Repairing Damaged Disks

One of the most valuable tools included in the Desktop package is the Norton Disk Doctor for Windows, a close cousin of the Norton Disk Doctor found in the Norton Utilities. The Disk Doctor for Windows checks critical areas of your disk for errors that may endanger your data and, if it finds errors, gives you the means to repair them.

In this step, you will use the Disk Doctor for Windows to check your hard disk. Since the program is largely automated, this step will only take about 15 minutes.

Running the Disk Doctor

To run the Disk Doctor for Windows and examine your disk, follow these steps:

1. With Full Menus enabled, pull down the Tools menu and select the Disk Doctor option. Unlike other Desktop tools, the Doctor occupies the entire screen, as in Figure 7.1.

2. On the Select Drives dialog window, click the C drive and then click OK. Note that it is possible to select multiple drives, and diagnose them all at once.

When you have made your drive selection, the Doctor begins work immediately, running six tests consecutively. It looks for errors in the following critical areas of your disk:

- Partition table: This is where DOS keeps information about the logical divisions on your hard disk. The partition table is not something the casual user has any contact with whatsoever. Many hard disks have a single partition encompassing the disk. This you see as drive C. Other hard disks, usually large ones, have two or more partitions. These most often appear to the user as multiple hard disks (C:, D:, E:, etc.). Multiple partitions also make it possible to load two operating systems on your computer—DOS

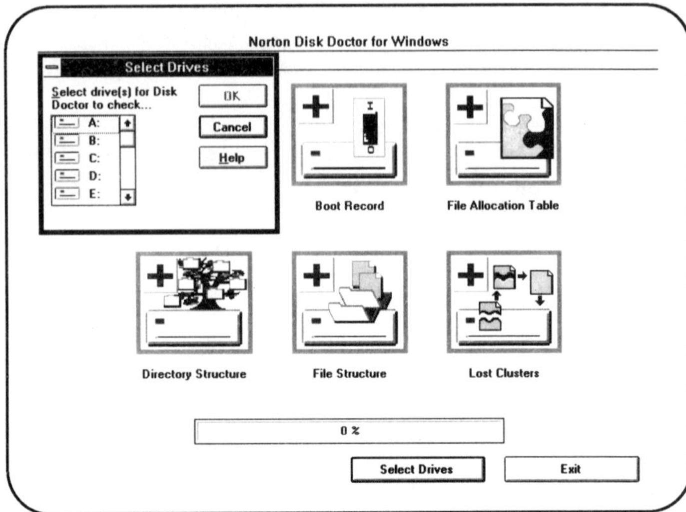

Figure 7.1: The Norton Disk Doctor for Windows

and OS/2 or DOS and UNIX, for example. Errors in the partition table endanger all data on your hard disk and usually manifest themselves as a sudden inability to boot your machine.

- Boot record: This area contains both information that DOS uses to boot and information about the physical layout of your hard disk. Though the boot record is not something the casual user ever meets, its integrity is necessary for booting your computer.
- File Allocation Table (FAT): DOS uses the FAT to keep track of every file on your disk. It is essentially a list matching individual clusters to the files that occupy them. Errors in the FAT can result in loss of data.
- Directory structure: This is what you see as the directory tree, and it is another device DOS uses to locate files on a disk. An error in a directory endangers every file contained in the directory.

- File structure: This test, unlike the four previous tests, does not check a physical entity. Instead it matches information in the directory structure against information in the FAT to make sure each file is where it is supposed to be.
- Lost clusters: This final test checks to see if there are any clusters on your disk that are "lost"—that seem to be part of a file but DOS can't tell which one. This is the error that the Doctor is most likely to find, and it is the least dangerous. Lost clusters don't often contain current data.

The Disk Doctor's Report

When the Doctor has finished running its tests, you will see a synopsis of its findings in the Test Results window, shown in Figure 7.2. The Disk Doctor also provides a more detailed, technical report, which you may wish to see, particularly if errors turn up. To see such a report, follow these steps:

1. Click the Info button on the Test Results window.
2. Click OK when you have finished reading. Click Print to send the report to the default printer, or click Save and enter a file name to save the report as a file on disk.

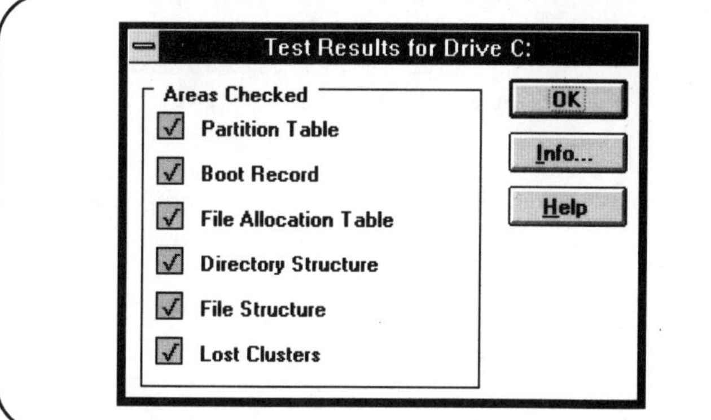

Figure 7.2: The Test Results window

Maintaining Your Disks

The Norton Disk Doctor can check floppy disks as well as hard disks. You should run it under the following circumstances:

- If a program reports that it is unable to read a file. Be careful here. Being unable to *read* a file is different from being unable to *find* a file. The former usually means that there is some kind of physical error involved. The latter simply means that the program in which you are working can't find the file you want.
- Once every few months on your older floppy disks and your hard disk as preventative maintenance.

Repairing Problems

Hopefully, the Disk Doctor did not find any errors on your hard disk. If this is the case, you can quit the Disk Doctor now. To do so, click Exit at the bottom of the screen to return to the Desktop (clicking Select Drives allows you to check another drive).

If, however, the Disk Doctor did find errors, you should repair them or have them repaired. The remainder of the step will show you how to use the Disk Doctor to do this. If you do not wish to do this by yourself, by all means get help, but do not leave the errors alone.

The Disk Doctor that you run from the Norton Desktop can only diagnose errors, it cannot repair them. To repair errors, you must run the Disk Doctor from the Emergency disk. Follow these steps:

1. Quit Windows and return to the DOS prompt.
2. Put the red Emergency disk in drive A.
3. Type

   ```
   a:ndd
   ```

   to start the program.

4. From the program's main menu, select the Diagnose Disk option.
5. On the list that appears, click on the drive letter of the drive you want to check. Then click the Diagnose option.
6. The Disk Doctor will rediagnose your hard disk until it comes across the error again. Explanations on errors and repairs are provided by the program, and the Doctor makes all fixes automatically. All that is left to the user is to select Continue in response to any explanation and to select Yes in response to any prompt to correct an error.

If the Disk Doctor is unable to fix an error it finds, you may have a serious problem with your hard disk or some other, related part of the computer. You should contact your dealer, manufacturer, or technical support department.

Running a Surface Test

Once the Disk Doctor runs its tests and repairs any damage, you can run a test which checks the surface of your hard disk for physical errors. As these crop up somewhat more often than the errors discussed above, it is a good idea to run it here. If the Disk Doctor finds any physical errors, it will mark the affected area so that it can no longer be used and thus present no danger to your data. If data is currently sitting on the affected area, it will be moved to a healthy section of the disk.

Before running the surface test, make sure you select the appropriate options. These options should be set according to Table 7.1.

Box	***Option to select***	***Purpose***
Test	Disk Test	Tests entire disk surface
Passes	Repetitions 1	Runs the surface test once (or the number of times specified here)

Table 7.1: Surface test options

Box	*Option to select*	*Purpose*
Test Type	Weekly	Provides a sufficiently rigorous test to catch incipient physical errors
Repair Setting	Repair Automatically	Automatically fixes any physical errors found

Table 7.1: Surface test options (continued)

Begin the surface test by selecting the Begin Test option at the bottom of the screen. When the surface test is finished (and any errors corrected) the Doctor displays a summary of its findings. If no errors were found, select the Done option.

If, however, errors were discovered, the summary information is available as a report. If the Doctor was unable to fix all errors, this report will be useful to anyone you contact for technical support. To print a report, select the Report option followed by the Print option. Select the Done option when the report is finished printing.

Having returned to the main program menu, select the Quit Disk Doctor option to return to the DOS prompt.

Step 8

Backing Up Your Data

The answer to the question "How often should I back up my data?" is "How much work do you want to do over again?" The simplest backup method, sufficient for most PC users, is to copy your data files to floppy disks each time you edit a file or create one anew. For users who deal in huge data files and large quantities of data, however, the "Floppy Copy" method is horribly inefficient, if not downright impossible. How do you copy a 4Mb database file onto floppy disk? For these users, the Norton Desktop provides the Norton Backup program. This program backs up all or part of your hard disk onto a series of floppies and can use these floppies to restore your data as necessary.

This step contains a tutorial on the Norton Backup in which you will back up your entire hard disk. Instructions will also be given for backing up only part of your hard disk and for restoring data. Depending on how much data you have on your hard disk, this step will take you anywhere from 30 minutes to one hour to complete.

Configuring Norton Backup

Before you begin, you should have some floppies ready. They do not have to be formatted (the Backup program will format them for you) and they do not have to be new (just make sure you are not using disks that have data you want to keep). The exact number you will need will be determined by the Backup program, but you should have approximately as many as will hold the amount of data on your hard disk (if your hard disk holds 10Mb of data, you should have ten high-density floppies). Once you have them together, number them.

Once you've gotten your floppies together, start the Backup program by pulling down the Tools menu and selecting Norton Backup or by double-clicking on the Backup icon. Since this is the first time you are running the Backup, it has not yet been configured. Follow these steps to have the Backup program configure itself automatically. You will only have to do this once. The next time you run the program, you will not have to do this and can back up your data right off.

1. When asked if you wish to create the setup file DEFAULT.SET, click Yes.
2. When asked if you wish to configure the program automatically, click Yes.
3. Click OK to allow compatibility testing.
4. Click OK to acknowledge that your floppy drive types have been set.
5. On the Configuration Tests dialog window, click Start. These tests ensure that the Backup will work reliably with your system.
6. Remove all disks from your floppy drives and click OK.
7. Click OK to acknowledge test results.
8. The Backup will now run a short test backup to make sure everything will work properly during a real backup. Put a disk in the indicated floppy drive (probably drive A) and click Start.
9. If drive A is not a 1.44Mb 3½-inch drive, you will need two disks to complete the test backup. Put disk #2 into drive A when prompted to do so. It is okay if the drive light is on when you swap disks.
10. When the test backup is finished, the program will compare data on the floppies with data on your hard disk to make sure the backup was done correctly. Put disk #1 back in drive A and click OK.
11. When prompted, put disk #2 in drive A.
12. Click OK to acknowledge the completion of data comparison and the end of automatic configuration.

Specifying Backup Options

Now that your hardware is properly configured, you can begin the process of backing up your hard disk. Click once on the large button marked Backup. The Backup window should appear, as in Figure 8.1.

Specifying Drives

On this screen, you must tell the Norton Backup exactly which hard drives are being backed up (if you have more than one) and which floppy drive you are using to do so, even if you only have one floppy drive. Again, this information is saved when you quit the program so future backup sessions will be properly configured from the start.

1. In the Backup From box, the default drive (most likely C) will already be selected. If it is not or if you have multiple hard drives, double-click on the drive(s) to be backed up. Selected drives are marked with a square.
2. In the Backup To box in the center of the Backup window, pull down the DOS Path list and select the floppy drive and the size of floppy disk you are using for the backup.

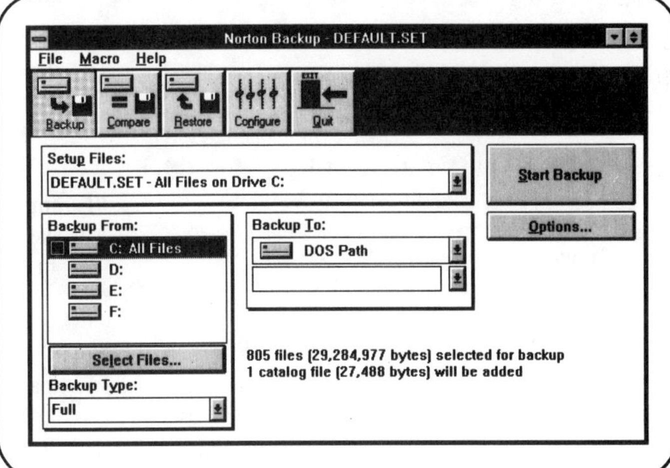

Figure 8.1: The Norton Backup window

At the bottom center of the Backup window, you will see exactly how many disks you will need, as well as how much data will be backed up and how long the process will take.

Specifying General Options

The last thing you should do before actually starting to back up is set a few general options, as these will make Backup work more efficiently.

1. Click Options. This brings up the Basic Backup Options dialog window.
2. You should make one change to the default settings here. Toggle on the Verify Backup Data option. This ensures that data is written correctly to the floppies.
3. Click OK.

Backing Up

You are now ready to begin the actual backup. Follow these steps:

1. Put floppy #1 in the backup drive.
2. Click Start Backup. This brings up the Backup Progress window, which you saw earlier during configuration. It is shown here in Figure 8.2. This window keeps you up to date on your backup. It shows you how much of the current floppy is full, what percentage of the operation is finished, how many disks you will need and have already used, and how much data has been and will be backed up.

If the floppy disk you use contains data, Backup will tell you so. If you are certain you don't need this data, click Overwrite. If you wish to keep the data, swap disks and click Retry.

3. When disk #1 is full, your computer will beep. Remove disk #1 and replace it with disk #2.
4. Repeat step 3 until the backup is finished.
5. Click OK to acknowledge completion.

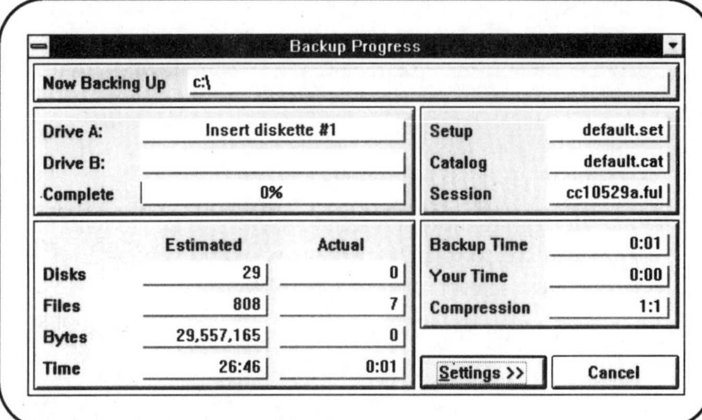

Figure 8.2: The Backup Progress window

Minimizing Backup

Because Norton Backup is a Windows program, you can run it while you are doing something else. Just minimize the Norton Backup and go about your business. When it comes time to swap disks, your computer will beep. If you do not respond to this first beep, Backup will beep again and pop up a window reminding you it is time to switch.

This brings you to the end of the tutorial. The remainder of the step will show you how to do a partial backup of your hard disk and how to restore data. While you can work along if you wish, it is probably not a good idea to restore data to your hard disk now. If you want to quit Norton Backup, click the large button marked Quit and then click OK to save current settings.

Partial Backup

Not everyone needs to back up their entire hard disk. More advanced users might find it useful to back up only some of their files. Follow these steps to do a partial backup:

1. Make sure you have set all options and configurations as instructed in the sections above.

2. Click Select Files. This brings up a screen like the one shown in Figure 8.3, with the directory tree of the selected drive in the left-hand panel and the files in the highlighted directory listed on the right.
3. Select only the files or directories you want to back up, keeping the following in mind:
   - By default all directories and all files contained therein are selected for backup. This is why a solid square appears next to each directory and file name.
   - To deselect a directory or a file name, double-click on its name (the solid square will disappear).
   - Double-clicking will also reselect a file or directory that is not selected.
   - You may find it useful to use the Select All and Deselect All options on the File menu to select or deselect the entire drive.
4. When you have made your selections, click OK.
5. Start your backup, following the steps in the "Backing Up" section above.

Restoring Data

A backup program would be of no use if it could not restore data to your hard disk. To restore data, follow these steps:

1. Start the Norton Backup.
2. Click the large button marked Restore.
3. At the Restore From prompt, make sure the floppy drive you used to back up your data is selected. If it is not, pull down the list and select the correct drive.
4. At the Restore Files prompt, double-click on the drive you are going to restore (if you backed up drive C, you will now restore drive C). Selected drives are marked with a square.

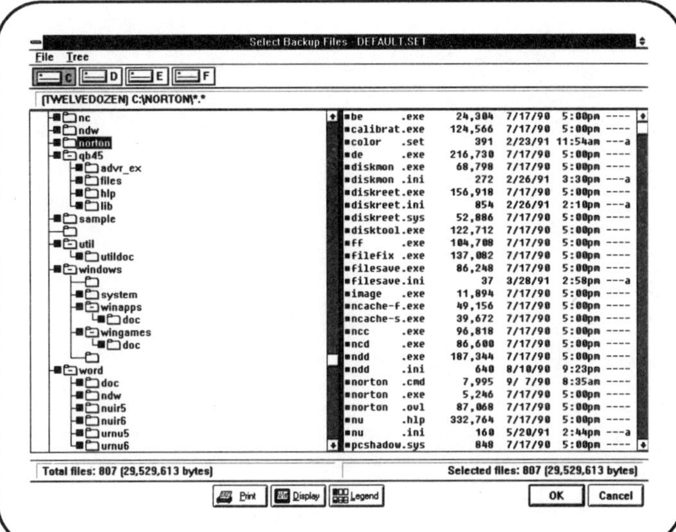

Figure 8.3: The Select Backup Files window

5. Click Options. This brings up the Basic Restore Options dialog window.
6. Toggle on the Verify Restored Files option and click OK; the default settings are otherwise acceptable. This option ensures that data restored to your hard disk is written without errors.
7. Place disk #1 in your floppy drive.
8. Click Start Restore. This brings up a Restore Progress window nearly identical to the Backup Progress window shown in Figure 8.2.
9. Switch floppies when you are prompted to do so until restoration is finished.
10. Click OK to acknowledge completion.

Step 9

Destroying Data

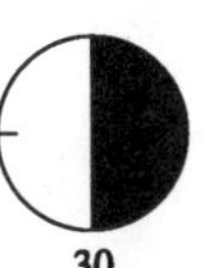

30

Occasionally it is necessary, for security reasons, to dispose of files in some permanent way. As you read in Step 6, simply deleting a file is insufficient because it does not actually delete a file's data from the disk; erased files can easily be unerased. By contrast, the Norton Shredder disposes of files by overwriting them.

Because the Shredder actually replaces your files with new and meaningless information, it is impossible to unerase shredded files, even when Erase Protect is active and TRASHCAN is working. You must be very sure, therefore, that you no longer need or want the information you are going to shred.

This step contains a tutorial on the Desktop's Shredder. You will learn how to shred individual files, entire directories, and even entire disks. It should take you about 30 minutes to complete.

Creating Sample Files

Before the tutorial begins, format a new floppy disk in drive A. It is important that you do not use one of your regular data disks or any other disk that holds information you need. Over the course of the tutorial, the entire disk will be shredded.

When you have formatted a new floppy, use the Windows Notepad to create four short sample files. Save them on this blank floppy with the names A:NINE.DOC, A:STEP9A.TXT, A:STEP9B.TXT, and A:STEP9C.TXT.

Shredding a File

Once the sample disk is prepared, you are ready to begin. To shred a single file, do the following:

1. With full menus enabled, pull down the Tools menu and select the Shredder option. The Shred window appears, as in Figure 9.1.

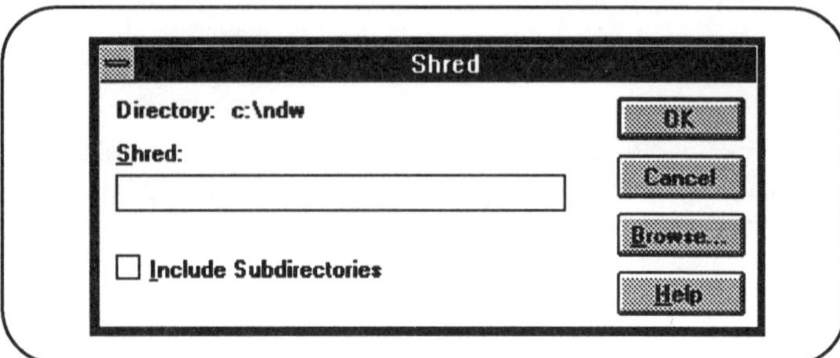

Figure 9.1: The Shred window

2. At the Shred prompt on the Shred window, type the name of the file you want to shred

   `a:step9a.txt`

   and click OK.

3. On the window warning that STEP9A.TXT will be permanently destroyed, click Yes twice.

The Shredder's progress is marked in the Shred Status window. When shredding is done, both the Shred window and Shred Status window will disappear.

Shredding Multiple Files

Using wildcards

If you had a number of files you wanted to dispose of, shredding them one at a time would be tedious. To shred more than one file in only one operation, you can use the above procedure with one minor modification. In step 2 of the procedure, enter a file specification using wildcards instead of just entering the name of one file. If, for example, you entered

`A:*.wk?`

you would shred all of the Lotus 1-2-3 files on the floppy in your A drive.

However, there will be circumstances where the files you wish to shred cannot be described by one file specification. The sample files NINE.DOC and STEP9B.TXT, for example, cannot be described using only one file specification. (Admittedly, you could shred both by using *.*, but this is no good if there are files you wish to keep among those you wish to shred.) To shred disparately named files in one operation, follow these steps:

1. Open the drive window for the drive on which the files reside. For the tutorial, open the A drive window by double-clicking on its icon.
2. Highlight the names of the files you want to shred (NINE.DOC and STEP9B.TXT) by holding down the Ctrl key and clicking on their names.
3. Pull down the Tools menu and select Shredder.
4. Click OK, and then Yes twice to shred each file when you are prompted for confirmation.

Shredding Directories

You can extend the above procedure to directories, thereby shredding the contents of an entire directory, or group of directories, all at once. Instead of selecting icons from the file list and activating the Shredder, you select directory icons, or "folders," from the directory tree.

To shred the remaining contents of the one directory on the sample disk, follow these steps:

1. The A drive window should still be open on your screen. Click on the root directory icon on the directory tree and select the Shredder option on the Tools menu.
2. Click OK, then Yes twice to confirm the deletion of STEP9C.TXT, the only file remaining on the sample disk.

Shredding multiple directories is, unsurprisingly, an extension of this procedure. You simply highlight them and select the Shredder option. To shred all files on a disk, you highlight all directories on the directory tree and select the Shredder option.

Note that shredding directories destroys the files contained within those directories, but it does not destroy the directories themselves.

An Alternate Shredding Method

The Shredder icon can be placed on the Desktop as well to shred files (and directories). To put the Shredder icon on the Desktop, select Preferences from the Configure menu. Then enable the Shredder option in the Tool Icons box and click OK. The Shredder icon appears on the Desktop. Instead of selecting the Shredder option on the Tools menu, you can drag file (or directory) icons onto the Shredder icon. Try this now.

1. Use the Windows Notepad again to create another sample file called A:STEP9D.TXT.
2. If the new file does not appear on the A drive window, pull down the View menu and select the Refresh option.
3. Drag the STEP9D.TXT icon from the A drive window onto the Shredder icon.
4. You should see the same confirmation box you saw while shredding files earlier. Click Yes twice to shred the sample file.

This brings you to the end of the tutorial. Close the A drive window and remove the sample disk from the drive. The remainder of the step is a brief discussion on configuring the Shredder. If shredding files is important to you, you should read on.

Configuring the Shredder

The Shredder works by overwriting the files or the space on your disk once with the character 0. If you wish to change the character used to overwrite data or the number of times data is overwritten, you can easily do so.

To configure the Shredder, pull down the Configure menu and select the Shredder option. The Configure Shredder dialog window appears, as in Figure 9.2. The meaning of each of the configuration options is listed below.

- US Government Shredding: Toggle this option on and the Shredder destroys data according to Department of Defense specifications. Data is alternately overwritten with the characters 0 and 1, three times each. Then the Shredder overwrites the data with ASCII character 246, the division sign (÷).
- Use Special Over-Write Pattern: Toggle this option on if you want to specify the character or characters with which data is overwritten. Type them in the box next to the option.
- Repeat: If you want to overwrite data more than once, type the number of repetitions here.

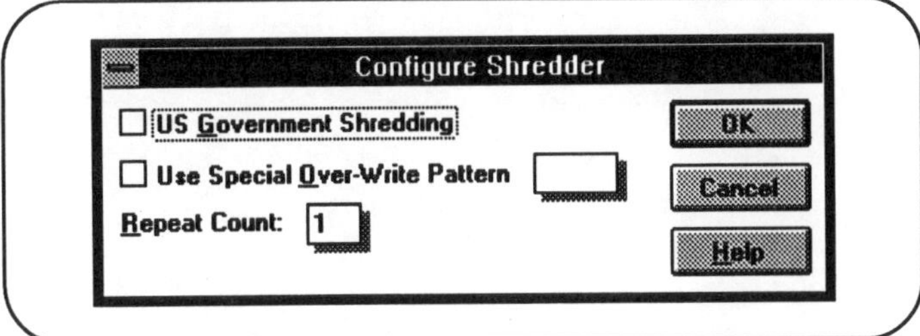

Figure 9.2: Shredder configuration options

Step 10

System Information

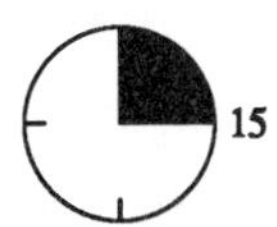

The Norton Desktop package provides a powerful diagnostic instrument in the System Info tool, which tells you nearly everything you ever wanted to know about your computer, both inside and out. This step presents a brief tutorial that takes you through some of the more accessible screens and shows you how to print out information. The screens not shown are summarized for your reference.

Running System Info

With Full Menus enabled, start System Info by pulling down the Tools menu and selecting the System Info option. When it starts, you will see the window shown in Figure 10.1.

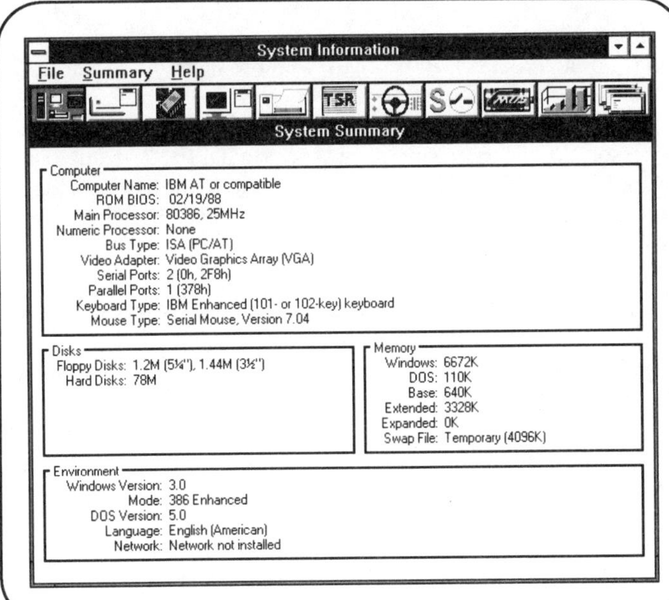

Figure 10.1: The System Summary window

The System Summary Window

The System Summary window always appears when you run System Info. It details the basic configuration of your computer. For example, the computer from which this image was taken is an 80386 machine running at 25 megahertz with no 80387 math coprocessor. It is running Windows 3.0 in 386 Enhanced mode and has VGA graphics and a serial mouse.

Above the System Summary information, you will see a row of icons, and above that, a menu bar. You can see the other information windows simply by clicking on their icons or by selecting them from the Summary pull-down menu. Let's move on to another information window.

The Processor Benchmark Window

CPU Speed

Click on the icon showing a 3D bar graph, or pull down the Summary menu and select the Processor Benchmark option. This brings up the Processor Benchmark window shown in Figure 10.2.

The bar graph in this window shows the speed of your main processor, the Compaq 386/33, and the original IBM AT relative to the speed of the IBM XT. As you can see, the AT is 4.4 times faster, the Compaq 34.7 times faster, and the machine from which this image was taken is 25.5 times faster.

Startup files

Finally, click on the icon showing cascading windows, or pull down the Summary menu and select the Startup Files option. This produces a set of five windows, each containing an important system file: AUTOEXEC.BAT, CONFIG.SYS, WIN.INI, SYSTEM.INI, and NDW.INI. Though you cannot edit these files here, this is an easy way to view their contents when you need to know what you've got or are considering making changes.

Remaining Information Windows

We will not step through the remaining eight windows, but they are summarized below as they appear left to right on the icon bar.

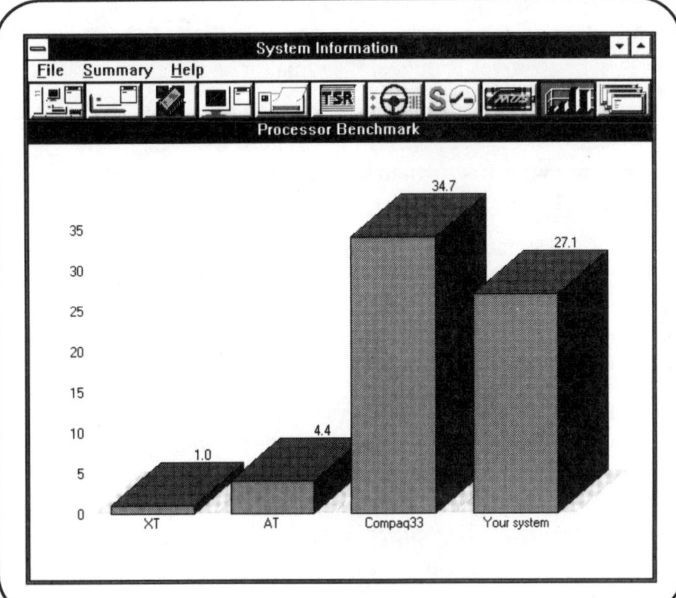

Figure 10.2: The Processor Benchmark window

- Disk Summary: Select the icon that depicts the front of a hard disk or select the Disk option from the Summary menu. This window shows information about all non-floppy drives installed on your system, volume names, current default directories, sizes, amounts of free and occupied space.
- Windows Memory: Select the icon that depicts a RAM chip or select the Windows Memory option from the Summary menu. This window shows how much memory is available to Windows and how much is currently being used by such things as applications and device drivers.
- Display Summary: Select the icon that depicts a video monitor or select the Display option from the Summary menu. This window gives detailed information about your display: the video card you use, your monitor type, its resolution in pixels, the number of pixels per inch.

- Printer Summary: Select the icon showing a printer or select the Printer option from the Summary menu. This window gives technical information on the active printer.
- TSR Summary: Select the icon with the letters *TSR* on it or select the TSR option from the Summary menu. This window shows the name, size, and memory address of all TSR's currently loaded.
- DOS Device Driver Summary: Select the icon depicting a steering wheel or select the Dos Device Drivers option from the Summary menu. This window gives the name, description, and memory address of all DOS device drivers loaded.
- Real Mode Software Interrupts: Select the icon with the large letter *S* and a switch or select the Real Mode Software Interrupts option from the Summary menu. This window lists current software interrupts. A software interrupt is the means by which a program lets the CPU know that it has an operation to carry out.
- CMOS Summary: Select the icon depicting a battery labeled CMOS, or select the CMOS option from the Summary menu. This window displays current settings stored in your CMOS. The CMOS is the means by which 286, 386, and 486 class machines remember what is installed on your computer (the kind of floppy disks, the amount of memory, the type and size of your hard disk).

Printing Information

If you would like to print out the information displayed in any or all of the System Info windows, it is a simple matter.

1. Pull down the File menu and select the Report Options option. This brings up the Report Options dialog window.
2. By default all printing options are toggled on. Leave on the options whose information you wish to print and click OK.
3. Pull down the File menu again and select Print Report.

Step 11

The Norton Screen Saver

45

You have probably seen screens on automatic teller machines or video games that have messages or images "burned" into them. On burnt screens, you can see a ghost of the message or image even when the screen is displaying something else. This image "burn-in" occurs when the same unvarying messages or images are displayed over a long period of time, many months or years. "Burn-in" can happen to your computer's monitor as well.

A screen saver program can delay the onset, or even prevent, monitor burn-in by blanking the screen or changing the display to a moving image after a specified period of inactivity. With a screen saver, if you leave your machine for hours at a time, there will be no fixed image displayed. Norton's screen saver, known as the Sleeper, comes with a variety of different screens you can use to save your display.

This step contains a tutorial in which you will sample the different screen saving images and learn to activate and configure the Sleeper. It should take you about 45 minutes to complete.

Sampling and Selecting Images

The Sleeper can only use one image at a time, though you have 13 to choose from. In this part of the tutorial, you will learn how to select and configure a saver image, while sampling all of them.

1. Start the Sleeper by pulling down the Tools menu and selecting the Sleeper option. This brings up the Norton Sleeper window shown in Figure 11.1. The box on the left-hand side of the window lists all of the screen saving images that come with the Sleeper.
2. Click once on Triquetrous Lights. Notice that the center box changes to show options for the selected image.
3. Click on Sample to see what Triquetrous Lights does to your screen. It looks something like a fireworks show. Notice that the Image Option box remains on the screen. It

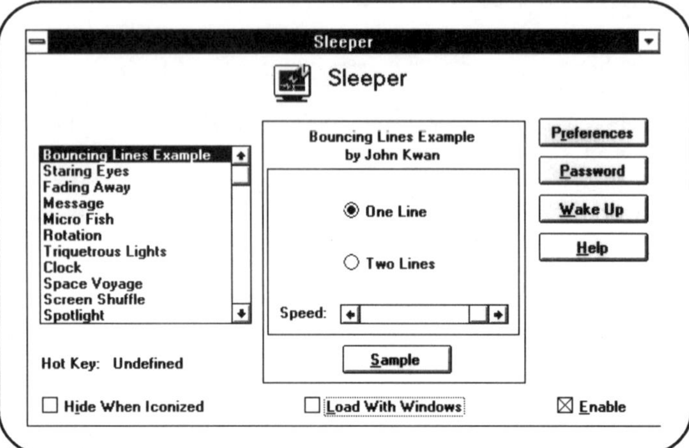

Figure 11.1: The Sleeper window

does so only because you are sampling the image. When the Sleeper is actually working, this box does not appear.

4. Click on Restore to "unblank" the screen and return to the Desktop.
5. Modify Triquetrous Lights by changing a few of its options.
6. Click Sample again to see what effect these options have.
7. When you have noted the differences, click Restore again.
8. Spend a while, even as much as a half hour, selecting and sampling each of the other images. After you have seen them all, select one that you particularly like for the remainder of the step.

Putting Your Screen to Sleep

Now that you have sampled each of the images and have selected one that you like, we will see the different ways the Sleeper can "blank" your screen when you are not working but your computer is on.

Activating the Sleeper

For the Sleeper to work, it first must be turned on. To activate the Sleeper, toggle on the Enable option in the bottom right corner of the Sleeper window if it is not already on.

While the Sleeper must be enabled to work, its window does not have to be open. In fact, most of the time the Sleeper is running, it will be minimized. However, to change any of the Sleeper's settings, its window must be open.

Sleeping Automatically

By default, the Sleeper will automatically put your screen to sleep if 55 minutes pass without your pressing a key or moving the mouse. This interval will be too long for some, such as word processors, who are typing more or less constantly, and too short for others, such as programmers who seem to stare endlessly into their screens. To change the amount of time the Sleeper will wait before blanking your screen, follow these steps:

1. Click the Preferences button on the Sleeper window.
2. At the top of the Preferences window, enter the number of minutes and seconds you want the Sleeper to wait and then click OK. For the moment, enter 0 minutes and 30 seconds.
3. Wait 30 seconds. The Desktop screen should disappear, and in its place you should see the save image you selected above. There should be no sample box this time.
4. Press a key to return to the Desktop.
5. Repeat steps 1 through 3 and set the Sleep interval to the time you will find most useful.

Sleeping Manually

The Sleep Now Corner

There will be times when you want to put your screen to sleep immediately, either because you are getting up from your computer or someone is looking over your shoulder. You can put your screen to sleep with the mouse by moving into a corner of the screen designated the Sleep Now Corner. If you'd rather use the keyboard, you need only press a designated sequence of keys. To specify the Sleep Now Corner, follow these steps:

1. Click the Preferences button on the Sleeper window.
2. At the bottom of the Preferences window, toggle on the Use Sleep Corners option, if it isn't on already. This is the option that allows you to blank the screen with the mouse.

3. On the Sleep Now Corner box, click the corner you want to use to put the screen to sleep and then click OK. You can designate any one of the four corners as the Sleep Now Corner. You may notice, however, that only three corners seem to be available. If you wish to use the fourth corner, you must change the selected Sleep Never Corner first. The Sleep Never Corner is explained below.
4. Move the mouse pointer all the way into the corner you designated as the Sleep Now Corner. The Desktop should disappear and your saver image should appear again.
5. Press a key or click or move the mouse to restore the Desktop.

The Sleep Never Corner

There will also be times when you don't want the screen to blank at all. If you're in the middle of a paper that requires a lot of thought, for example, you don't want to be distracted by your computer's putting on a light show all of a sudden. If you move your mouse into the Sleep Never Corner, the Sleeper will never blank your screen, even if the designated amount of time for blanking the screen passes. You can change the Sleep Never Corner by following the steps above and clicking the corner you want in the Sleep Never Corner box.

Sleep keys

To put the display to sleep using the keyboard, you press a key combination that you have designated as hot keys. To specify your hot-key combination, follow these steps:

1. Click the Preferences button on the Norton Screen Saver window.

2. On the Preferences window, toggle on the Use Sleep Hot Keys option if it isn't on already, and then click OK.
3. Click once in the Select Hot Keys box.
4. Press the key combination you will use to blank the screen and then click OK.

Your key combination must use the Ctrl or the Ctrl and Alt keys together with a letter, number, or direction key.

5. Put the screen to sleep by pressing your hot keys.
6. Return to the Desktop by pressing any key or moving or clicking the mouse.

Password Protection

You may, if you wish, frustrate prying eyes by requiring a password to wake the screen. Note, however, that this is not a great security measure, as rebooting the machine is sufficient to get around it. To specify the password needed to unblank the screen, follow these steps:

1. Click the Password option on the Sleeper window.
2. Select the Custom Password option, and then click once in the adjacent text box. Delete the asterisks and type the password you want to use, and click OK.
3. Confirm the password you entered by retyping it and clicking OK.

If you wish to turn off the password, repeat step 1 above, but select the No Password option on the Password window. You must then enter your (old) password to confirm the change. Then click OK.

Running the Sleeper Automatically

This brings you to the end of the Sleeper tutorial. If you have been working along, the Sleeper should be running and configured as you want it.

When you restart Windows and the Norton Desktop, you must also restart the Sleeper from the Tools menu if you want to use it. This can be inconvenient if you want it for everyday use. Fortunately, you can configure the Sleeper to start automatically when you run Windows. To do so, toggle on the Load With Windows option at the bottom of the Sleeper window. You need to do this only once.

Step 12

Calculators

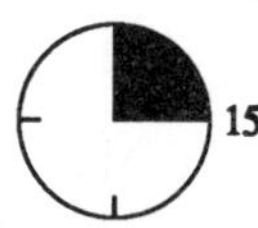

The Norton Desktop provides two calculators for your convenience: a ten-key, ordinary looking calculator (tape calculator), and a scientific calculator. Because of space limitations, this step cannot go into detail about the functions found on the calculators, but it will show you the fundamentals of using them. It should take you about 15 minutes to complete.

The Ten-Key Calculator

The ten-key calculator is useful for basic computation. To start it, first enable Full Menus and then pull down the Tools menu and select the Calculator option. When you start the Desktop calculator for the first time, the ten-key comes up by default. If the scientific calculator is on screen, pull down its Calculator menu and select the Tape option.

Pressing the Buttons

You can operate the ten-key with the mouse or with the keyboard. When using the mouse, simply click once on the button you wish to "press." The calculators may, however, be the only Desktop programs that are easier to use with the keyboard, simply by virtue of what you do with them.

When using the keyboard, you generally press the key that has the same letter, number, or symbol as the calculator button you wish to press. For example, press **T** for the total key, **5** for the number 5, or **M** and + for Memory Plus.

Other keys have an underlined letter. To press these from the keyboard, hold down the Ctrl key and press the underlined letter. Ctrl-E presses Clear Entry, for example.

Finally, a few buttons are not represented on the keyboard nor do they have an underlined letter. These buttons and the keys that press them are listed in Table 12.1.

Calculator Key	*Name*	*Keyboard Equivalent*
+/–	Change Sign	\
*	Multiplication	*
÷	Division	/
TXT	Text	Shift-"

Table 12.1: Unusual keyboard equivalents

Proper Operations

If you have ever used a ten-key calculator before, you probably already know the proper way to enter mathematical operations.

Addition and subtraction

For addition and subtraction, each number must be entered with the plus or minus keys and the sum or difference obtained with the Total key. The = key is not used. This may seem a bit abstract for simple addition, but what it means is this. To solve 138 – 59, you would enter

```
138
+
59
-
```

and click T to get the proper answer, 79. If one were to enter

```
138
-
59
T
```

this would produce –138. This is because the second number, 59, was not assigned a positive or negative operator, so it was not entered. Thus the total key had only the first number to operate on.

Multiplication and division

For multiplication and division, the proper key sequence is a bit more intuitive. To solve 138 x 59, for example, you would enter

```
138
*
59
=
```

to get the proper answer, 8142, as shown in Figure 12.1.

The Tape

As you work with the ten-key, all of its operations appear on the tape. The tape's contents can be printed or saved as a file. In

Figure 12.1: The tape calculator

addition, the contents of the calculator's display line can be copied to the Windows Clipboard for transfer to other applications. To copy the contents of the display line to the Clipboard, pull down the ten-key's Edit menu and select the Copy option. The ten-key's remaining functions are all found on its File menu. These functions are summarized in the list below.

- Open Tape: Restores a saved tape to the ten-key.
- Print Tape: Prints the current tape or any saved tape.
- Save Tape: Saves the current tape to file.
- Save Tape As: Saves the current tape under a different file name.

The Scientific Calculator

The Desktop's scientific calculator is really a programmer's and engineer's calculator. It handles all basic operations, algebraic and trigonometric functions, and conversions between decimal and hexidecimal numbers.

To switch from the ten-key calculator to the scientific, pull down the ten-key's Calculator menu and select the Scientific option. If you have already entered data on the ten-key (tape) calculator, you will be asked if you want to save the tape in a file.

Pressing the Buttons

Like the ten-key, the scientific calculator can be used with either the mouse or the keyboard. When using the mouse, simply click once on the button you wish to press. When using the keyboard, there are two considerations. If the button you wish to press has an exact match on the keyboard, press that key. For example, type **8** to press the number eight button, press Alt to press the Calculator's Alt key, and so on. Buttons with no exact match have a capitalized and underlined letter in their name indicating the corresponding key. Press **T** for the Tan (tangent) key or press **G** for the loG (logarithm) key, for example. Pressing the Ctrl key with the underlined letter is not necessary.

Shifted keys

Almost every key on the scientific calculator has a second function, listed directly above the button. To access a key's second function, first press the Alt key, then press the key whose second function you want. For example, to enter pi, press the Alt key and then the 0 key.

Proper Operations

Because the scientific calculator uses Reverse Polish Notation, entering an operation is different on the scientific calculator from on the ten-key. If you know Reverse Polish Notation, you probably find it more efficient than standard ten-key operation, particularly for long operations. If you don't know it, you might find it a bit confusing. The first number in an operation is followed by the Enter key. Subsequent numbers are followed by the operators. To calculate the multi-operator equation

(4 x (130 + 8)) / 12

you would enter

```
130
Enter
8
+
4
*
12
/
```

to produce 46. A total of 11 keystrokes were used. If, by contrast, you were to use the ten-key calculator to solve this equation, it would take 14 keystrokes.

```
130
+
8
+
T
*
```

```
4
=
/
12
=
```

If you would like more information about Reverse Polish Notation or the individual functions of the scientific calculator, please consult the Help menu or the Norton Desktop program manuals.

Step 13

KeyFinder

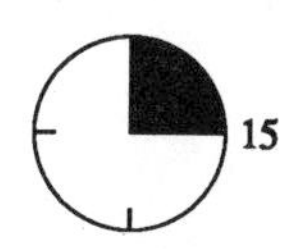

One of the more useful of the smaller tools included in the Norton Desktop package is the KeyFinder. It is essentially a sophisticated ASCII table that provides information about and access to all of the characters included in the fonts you have installed in Windows. If you frequently use characters not found on the keyboard—whether because you use foreign words in your documents or because you program—you will like KeyFinder.

This step will take you on a quick tour of the KeyFinder. It should take you about 15 minutes to complete.

Starting KeyFinder

To start the KeyFinder program, pull down the Tools menu and select the KeyFinder option. This brings up the KeyFinder window, shown in Figure 13.1. You will see the characters of the currently selected font (System) laid out in a grid occupying most of the window. The currently selected character appears in a box in the upper right corner of the window.

Different Fonts and Font Sizes

Different fonts

The different fonts available to you are listed in the Available Fonts box in the lower right side of the KeyFinder window. These fonts include those that come with Windows, any that you have installed through the Windows Control Panel, and any soft fonts that are part of Adobe Type Manager or any similar program that you have installed. To select a different font, simply click once on its name.

As you experiment with selecting different fonts, notice that all fonts do not contain the same set of characters. Some, in fact, will be missing entire segments of the standard ASCII set of 256 characters. These missing segments will appear as a run of dots, blocks, or blank spaces.

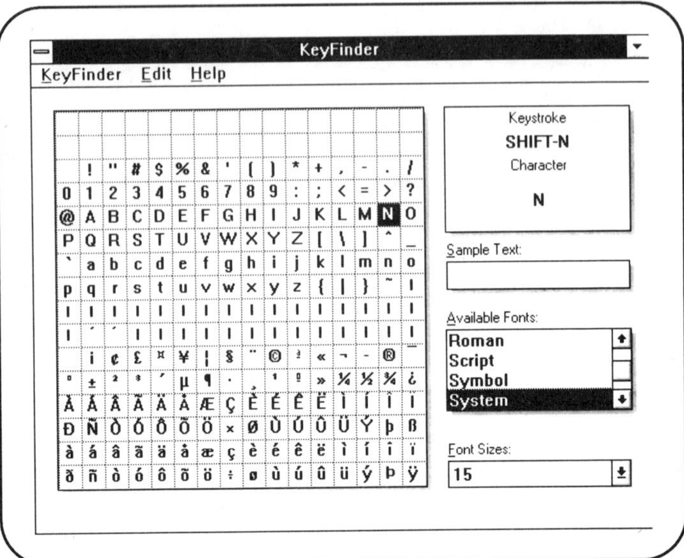

Figure 13.1: The KeyFinder

Different font sizes

Each font is probably available in more than one size. The sizes available for each font are found in the Font Sizes pull-down list. Select a number of different sizes for some different fonts now, and as you do so, watch the current character in the upper right corner change size and appearance.

Selecting and Generating Characters

The box in which the current character is displayed also shows the keystrokes that will produce this character in your applications. For any character on the keyboard, you already know the proper keystrokes; Shift-N, for example, produces an uppercase *N*. But what about characters that are not on the keyboard? Let's say you are typing a business letter in Times Roman and need to use the copyright symbol (©). To put the copyright symbol into your letter, open the KeyFinder and follow these steps:

1. Click once on Tms Rmn in the Available Fonts box to bring up the Times Roman font.

2. Click once on the copyright symbol.

The copyright symbol appears in the KeyFinder's upper right corner, along with the key sequence ALT-0169.

This tells you that by holding down the Alt key and typing

```
0169
```

on the numeric keypad (*not* the numbers across the top of your keyboard, and no need to turn on NUMLOCK either), you will enter the copyright symbol directly into your document.

Remember that the fonts displayed in KeyFinder are Windows fonts and as such are accessible only in Windows applications. Typing Alt-0169 in a non-Windows application is likely to result in another character entirely.

Cutting and Pasting Characters

You can also enter characters not on the keyboard by cutting or copying them from the KeyFinder to the Windows Clipboard and then pasting them into your document. Say you were typing a paper and needed to type the name of the sixteenth-century German mystic Jakob Böhme, complete with umlaut over the *o*. To cut and paste this name, or any other character or characters into your document, you would do the following:

1. Start KeyFinder.
2. Click once on Tms Rmn in the Available Fonts box to bring up the Times Roman font.
3. Double-click on each of the letters B-ö-h-m-e. This causes the name to appear, one letter at a time, in the Sample Text box above the Available Fonts box.
4. Highlight the name in the Sample Text box.
5. Pull down the Edit menu and select the Copy option. This copies the name to the Windows Clipboard.

6. Return to your word processor and paste the name in (usually by pulling down the Edit menu and selecting the Paste option).

Programmer Mode

KeyFinder's usefulness as a reference tool goes beyond being a simple ASCII table from which you can cut and paste characters. It also gives hexadecimal and octal equivalents for each character (the character's ASCII number in Base 16 and Base 8 notations), making it useful as a programmer's tool. To switch the KeyFinder into programmer mode, pull down the KeyFinder menu and select the Programmer Mode option. This changes the KeyFinder display in the following ways (see Figure 13.2):

- The Font Sizes box is turned off.
- The grid is now numbered in hexadecimal. You can get the hexadecimal number for each character, therefore, just by looking at its place in the grid.

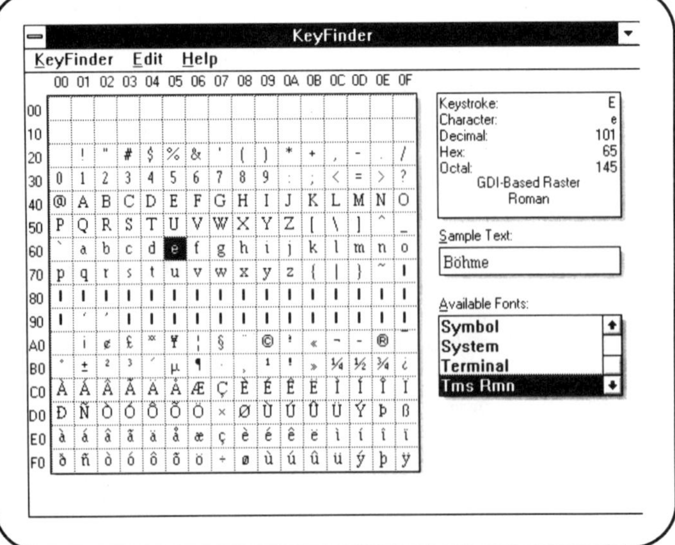

Figure 13.2: The KeyFinder in programmer mode

- The information about the currently selected character has been expanded to include its hexadecimal and octal equivalents.

Finishing Up

This brings you to the end of the KeyFinder tour. If you find KeyFinder useful, consider starting it automatically when you start the Desktop. Drag the KeyFinder icon from the NDW group into the AutoStart group to do so. For now, quit the program by pulling down the KeyFinder menu and selecting the Exit option.

Step 14

Editing Icons

Many Windows users get the urge, at one time or another, to tinker with their icons. With the Icon Editor program, the Norton Desktop provides the means to satisfy this urge. The Icon Editor is essentially a paint program for icons: You can use it to put your own, personal stamp on existing icons or you can create icons anew.

This step will expose you to the fundamentals of the Icon Editor, and as experimentation is encouraged, it should take about one hour to complete.

Running the Icon Editor

Begin the tutorial by starting the Icon Editor. With Full Menus enabled, pull down the Tools menu and select the Icon Editor option. The Icon Editor appears, as in Figure 14.1.

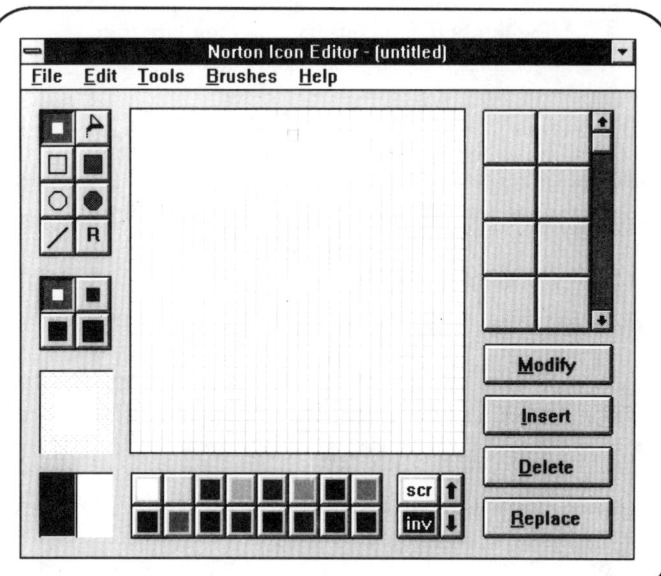

Figure 14.1: The Icon Editor

The Color Palette

No matter what operation you perform in the Icon Editor, you will begin by selecting colors from the Color Palette. The Color Palette consists of the 16 colored buttons arranged in two rows across the bottom of the Icon Editor window. To the left of these buttons, in the very bottom left of the window, is the color assignment display. By default, black is assigned to the left mouse button and white to the right. Thus the left panel of the display is black and the right panel is white.

Move the mouse pointer onto the work grid at the center of the window and click the left button once. The square under the pointer turns black. Now click the right button on the same square and it changes to white.

Changing colors

To change the colors assigned to the mouse buttons, simply click once on the button with the color you want. Click the left mouse button on red and the right button on dark blue and watch the color display change accordingly. Now, select two squares on the work grid. Click the left button on one and the right button on the other. This should produce one red square and one blue square.

Unlike most paint programs, the Icon Editor does not assign different functions to the two mouse buttons. Both perform the same function, but in different colors. Thus you always work with two colors at your immediate disposal (though, of course, you can assign the same color to both buttons if you wish).

The Grid

If it isn't already clear, all editing takes place on a 32 x 32 square grid at the center of the Icon Editor window. Since Windows icons are, by convention, 32 pixels square, each square on the grid represents one pixel in the icon. As it is often difficult to tell how your edits will appear in their actual size, the icon is displayed in its actual size in the display immediately above the color assignment display. Keep an eye on the icon display as you experiment with the editing tools in the next section.

Tools

The Icon Editor provides eight editing tools, laid out in two rows of four buttons in the upper left corner of the Icon Editor Window. You select a tool simply by clicking once on the appropriate button. We will experiment with each tool in turn.

The Brush

The brush is the tool selected by default when you start the Icon Editor; you used it briefly above. You select the brush by clicking the button, currently depressed, depicting a small central square. The brush's name is derived from "paintbrush," which is what the analogous tool is called in other paint programs.

You use the brush much as you would a paintbrush or a pencil: simply drag the brush across the area where you wish to make a mark. Move the mouse pointer onto the grid—notice that the pointer changes to a small square—and click either mouse button. Now hold the mouse button down while dragging the pointer. Notice that each square over which the pointer passes is colored.

The Filler

The filler is selected with the button depicting an overturned flask pouring liquid. It is used to fill up an area of the workspace in one quick operation. Note that the area you intend to fill must be completely enclosed, otherwise the color will "leak," coloring every square on the grid that you have not previously colored yourself.

Try the filler now. With the brush still selected, draw a small, enclosed shape. Select the filler tool and a new color, then fill the shape.

Rectangles

There are two rectangle tools, selected by the buttons in the second row of tools: a large, empty square and an identically sized filled square. As you might well imagine, the former allows you to draw a hollow rectangle, while the latter draws a solid one.

Try drawing some rectangles now. First select two new colors to use; don't worry about drawing over some of your previous experiments. Now select the hollow rectangle tool. Move the mouse pointer over the grid and notice that the pointer turns into a cross. When you are at a spot where you want to place a corner of the rectangle, click and hold the mouse button. Then drag the pointer to a square diagonally opposite the first corner. Notice the rectangle's shadow expanding as you go. When you reach the point where you want to place the opposite corner, let go of the button and the rectangle will appear.

The procedure for drawing filled rectangles is the same—just use the other rectangle tool.

Ellipses

There are two tools for drawing ellipses, selected by clicking on the buttons in the third row of tools: the hollow and filled circles.

The procedure for drawing ellipses is the same as that for drawing rectangles. Select two new colors and then select one of the ellipsis tools. The pointer is a cross when placed over the grid and you drag it from "corner" to "corner," creating a shadow rectangle as you go. When you let go of the mouse button, an ellipsis will be inscribed in the shadow rectangle.

Lines

To select the tool for drawing lines, press the button showing a diagonal line. Again the pointer becomes a cross when above the grid. Click and hold at one end of the line and drag the pointer to where you wish to place the other end. As you are dragging, a shadow line appears. The real line appears when you let go of the button.

The Replacer

This tool is selected with the button showing the letter *R*. Called a color eraser in other programs, the Replacer is a brush that allows you to change one color into another while leaving everything else on the workspace untouched.

To use the Replacer, first press the R button. Then, select one color you have previously used, say dark blue, and one you have not yet used, say dark gray. Move the pointer over the grid—it changes to a square brush—and click and hold the button assigned gray. Any time the brush touches a dark blue square, the square turns dark gray. All other colors are unaffected.

Notice that the Replacer also works backward. You can change dark gray to dark blue by clicking and dragging the other button, the one assigned to dark blue.

Brush Sizes

Below the Tools buttons on the Icon Editor window there is an arrangement of four buttons, each depicting a square of a different size. These are the different size brushes. The default brush, which you have been working with up to this point, is the 1 pixel x 1 pixel brush. It colors one square at a time on the grid, it draws a line one square wide, and it draws hollow shapes with borders one square wide. The next size is 2 x 2. When used with the brush it fills 2 x 2 squares on the grid (i.e., four squares total), draws lines two squares wide, and so on. The two remaining sizes are 3 x 3 and 4 x 4, which work like the 2 x 2 brush size but for those larger dimensions. Experiment with brush sizes now.

Erasing and Undoing

Unlike other paint programs, the Icon Editor does not provide an eraser tool. However, you can easily use the brush in this capacity. Simply select the current background color, white by default, and brush over the area you want to erase.

The Icon Editor does, however, have the capacity to undo mistakes. To undo your last edit, simply pull down the Edit menu and select the Undo option.

Your last edit is defined as anything you have written to the workspace since you last changed tools or brush sizes. For example, if you were to draw four hollow rectangles one after another using the same size brush, selecting the Undo option would remove them all. By contrast, if you were to draw a hollow rectangle followed by a line, selecting the Undo option would only erase the line.

If you happen to be dissatisfied with everything you have drawn, you can erase the entire workspace. Simply pull down the Edit menu, select the Clear Workspace option, and click OK to confirm the erasure.

File Formats Supported

The Icon Editor allows you to edit three different kinds of icon files: program files (.EXE files), individual icon files (.ICO files), and icon library files (.NIL files), created by the Icon Editor.

Editing Icons in .EXE Files.

Every program written for Windows will contain one or more icons, and you can edit any of these icons with the Icon Editor. Since the Program Manager file (PROGMAN.EXE) contains a number of icons you are probably familiar with, we'll practice editing Program Manager icons. If you want to change one or more icons in this or any other Windows program (.EXE) file, follow these steps:

1. Pull down the File menu and select the Open option.
2. At the File Type prompt on the dialog box that appears, select Executable.
3. Then, in the directory list box immediately above, double-click on the directory in which the file you want resides. In this case, to get to the C:\WINDOWS directory, double-click on [-c-], double-click on [..] until it disappears from

the list, and then double-click on [windows], scrolling the list if necessary.

4. On the file list box, scroll the list and click once on the name of the file you want (PROGMAN.EXE), and then click OK. All icons contained in the file will then appear in the Icon Editor's icon list, as in Figure 14.2. Note that only eight icons can be displayed in the list at once. You can scroll the list down to see more.
5. From the icon list, click the icon you want to edit and then click Modify. The icon will appear in the workspace.
6. Make your edits on the workspace, keeping an eye on the icon display to see how your edits will look in their actual size.

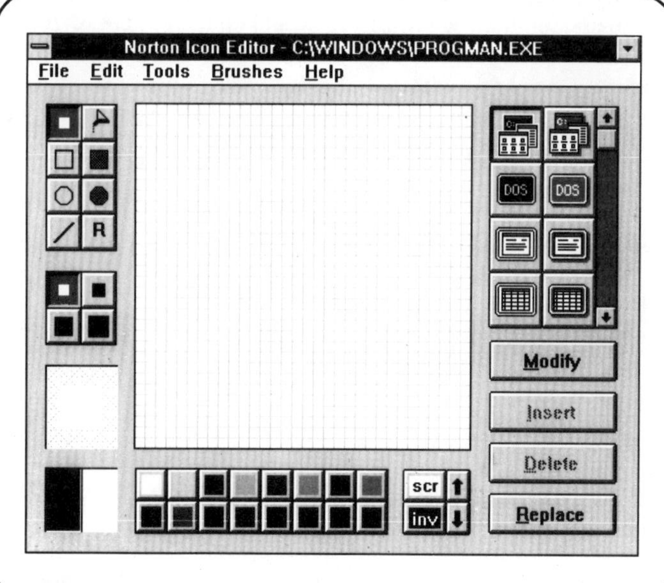

Figure 14.2: The Icon Editor's icon list

7. When you are finished editing the icon, click Replace. This replaces the selected icon on the icon list with the contents of the workspace.
8. Repeat steps 3–7 to change any of the other icons on the list.
9. When you have finished, pull down the File menu and select the Save option to save your work.

Your new icon will not, however, be immediately visible on the screen. If you look, you will still see the old, seemingly unchanged icon. To put your new edited icon in place of the old, follow the steps under "Replacing Icons" below.

Icon Libraries

An icon library is a file created by the Icon Editor that contains icons only. Icon libraries have the extension .NIL. You can modify any icon in an icon library, just as you would an icon in an .EXE file. You can also add icons to and remove icons from an icon library, which you cannot do with an .EXE file. To edit the contents of an icon library, you follow the same steps as for editing an .EXE file, except that the file type you select will be .NIL.

To add an icon to an icon library, simply make a new icon, click Insert, and save the file. Insert adds the contents of the workspace to the icon library. To delete an icon from an icon library, select the icon you wish to remove from the icon list, click it, and then click Delete. The icon will disappear from the icon list. You will then need to save your library file.

Icon Files

An icon file (.ICO) is a standard Windows icon file format. Unlike icon libraries, it contains one and only one icon.

When you are creating a new icon that you intend to save in the .ICO format, you must be careful of one thing. The Icon Editor by default will save a new icon in the .NIL format. Before you create a new icon file, pull down the File menu and select the New option. On the dialog window that appears, select the Icon option and click OK. This disables the Icon Editor's library functions and will save your new icon in the .ICO format.

Replacing Icons

You can use any icon to represent any program you are running under the Desktop. The format in which your "replacement" icon is stored does not matter. You can use icons from an icon library (.NIL), from an icon file (.ICO) or even from another program (.EXE). To replace one icon with another, follow these steps:

1. Open the group containing the icon you wish to replace. Click once on this icon.
2. Pull down the File menu and select the Properties option. You will see the original icon at the top of the dialog window that appears.
3. Click the Icon option.
4. Click once in the Icon File box and type the name of the file containing your replacement icon. Make sure to include the path.
5. Click the View button.
6. Pull down the Icon(s) list. All of the icons in the file specified in step 4 will be visible.
7. Click on the icon you want as a replacement.
8. Click OK twice.

The replacement icon now appears in the group window.

Step 15

The Scheduler

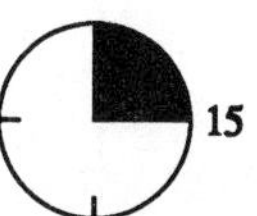

The Scheduler tool is a variation on standard appointment calendar programs. Like most calendar programs, it can give you detailed reminders at a specified time or at regular intervals. Unlike most calendar programs, however, the Scheduler can also run other programs for you at a specified time or at regular intervals.

This step contains a short tutorial in which you will learn how to schedule a reminder and schedule automatic program execution. It should take you about 15 minutes to complete.

A Sample Reminder

Let's start the tutorial by scheduling a reminder. Follow these steps:

1. Start the Scheduler program by pulling down the Tools menu and selecting the Scheduler option. This brings up the Scheduler window, as in Figure 15.1. The Events list shows one event, the daily backup you were asked about during installation. You can delete this or keep it and use it regularly. Instructions for both options are at the end of this step.
2. Click Add. This brings up the Add Event window shown in Figure 15.2.
3. In the box under the Description prompt, type a description of the reminder:

   ```
   Reminder test - event 1
   ```

   The description allows you to tell events apart when they are all listed together in the Scheduler window.
4. In the Type of Action box, click the Display Message option.

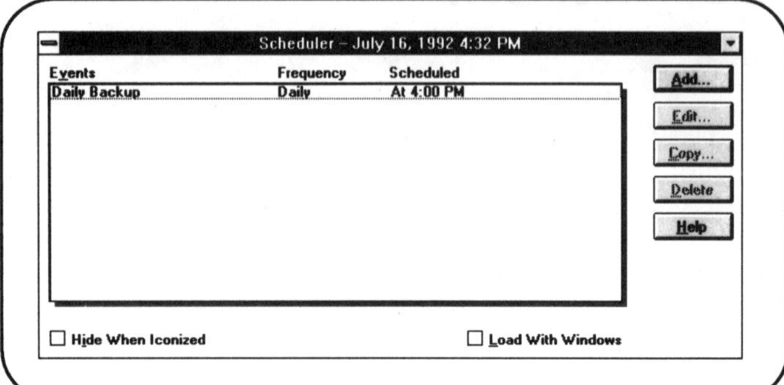

Figure 15.1: The Scheduler window

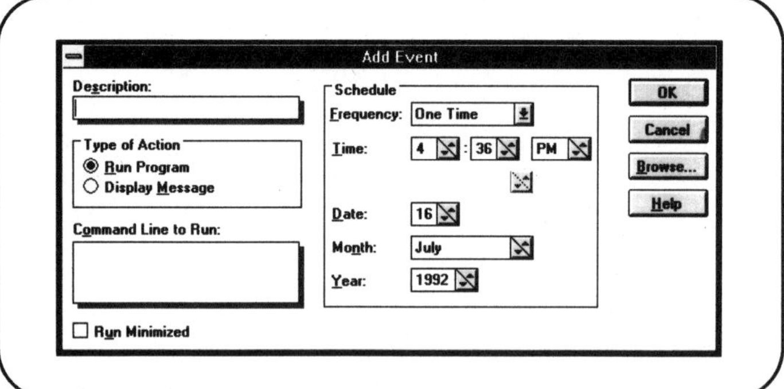

Figure 15.2: The Add Event window

5. Click in the box under the Message to Display prompt. Now type the actual reminder text:

   `When you are done working through Step 15, go on to Step 16.`

Now, in the Schedule box, you must specify how often and when this reminder will appear.

1. Leave the Frequency option at One Time, as this reminder will happen once and once only. Other frequency options,

which can be selected from the pull-down list, are explained below.

2. Since this reminder will occur only once, you must specify the exact date and time you want it to appear. Leave the Date, Month, and Year prompts alone, as they show today's date.
3. Though the current time is kept on the Scheduler title bar, it is not updated when the Add Event window is active. To see the current time up to the minute, run and minimize the Windows clock (found in the Accessories group).
4. Click the small up arrow to increment the minutes to two minutes after the current time, so the reminder will go off in a bit.
5. Click OK and the reminder will appear on the Scheduler's Events list.

Wait a little and then your computer will beep and you will see a dialog window displaying the sample reminder and its description. Click OK to acknowledge and close the reminder. Note that the reminder, once executed, disappears from the Events list.

Scheduling Frequencies

In addition to one-time reminders, the Scheduler can produce reminders at different regular intervals. This makes it useful for scheduling regular appointments and meetings. The other Frequency options are listed and detailed in the Table 15.1 below.

Frequency Option	*Executes Reminder*	*You Need to Set the...*
One Time	Once only	Hour, Minute, Meridian, Date, Month, Year
Hourly	Once per hour	Minute
Daily	Once per day	Hour, Minute, Meridian

Table 15.1: Scheduler Frequencies

Frequency Option	*Executes Reminder*	*You Need to Set the...*
Weekdays	Once per day, Mon.–Fri.	Hour, Minute, Meridian
Weekly	Once per week	Hour, Minute, Meridian, Day
Monthly	Once per month	Hour, Minute, Meridian, Date

Table 15.1: Scheduler Frequencies (continued)

Running a Program with Scheduler

In addition to providing reminders, the Scheduler can automatically run programs at specified times. This can be very useful, for example, if you check your e-mail as soon as you arrive in the office in the morning.

In this second part of the tutorial, you will set the Scheduler to run the Icon Editor. Note that the procedure is nearly identical to the procedure for setting reminders.

1. On the Scheduler window, click Add. This brings up the Add Event window again.
2. In the Description box, enter a description again:

   `Program Test - Event 2`

3. In the Type of Action box, click the Run Program option.
4. Click in the Command Line to Run box and type the file name and path of the program to run:

   `c:\ndw\iconedit.exe`

5. In the Schedule box, again leave the Frequency option at One Time and increment the minute to two minutes after the current time.
6. Click OK.

Now after two minutes' wait, the Icon Editor window should appear. The Icon Editor was chosen here for no particular reason. You can have the Scheduler run any program, Windows application or non-Windows application.

Useful Scheduler Features

This brings you to the end of the tutorial. Before you close the Scheduler window, take note of the following:

- Unlike one-time events, regular events will remain on the Events list. If you wish to remove an event manually, highlight the event in question and click Delete.
- If you want to modify a listed event, for example, because your schedule changes, highlight it on the list and click Edit. The dialog window for editing an event is the same as the window for adding an event. Follow the relevant steps in the sections above if you need guidance.
- Occasionally, the time designated for a one-time event will pass when your computer is off. When you next start the Scheduler, it will give you the option of purging such expired events, lest they clutter your Events list.
- If you are going to use the Scheduler on a regular basis, it would be inconvenient to start it every time you turn on your machine. To make the Scheduler start automatically when you start Windows, toggle on the Load With Windows option before you close the program. You will only need to do this once.

Step 16

Customizing the Desktop

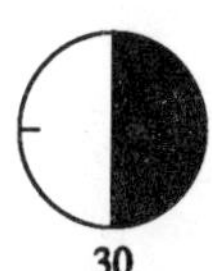
30

If the on-screen workspace of the Norton Desktop is not arranged to your liking, you can customize it to suit your own work habits. This step shows you how to have Norton Desktop programs appear as icons on the Desktop, how to change the location of the drive icons, and how to change the buttons on the drive window button bar. You will also learn how to turn off the confirmation of file operations (the "Are you sure?" messages that ask you to confirm that you really want to delete a file, for instance) and assign shortcut keystroke combinations to frequently used menu commands.

Configuring Preferences

Norton makes certain assumptions about the optimal Desktop for most people. However, part of what makes the Desktop such an enhancement to Windows is the extent to which it allows you to change the way your on-screen workspace is arranged. Most of these changes can be made from the Configure menu on the Desktop.

We will start with the Preferences settings. With Full Menus enabled, select Preferences from the Configure menu. You will see the window shown in Figure 16.1.

The Prompt for Filename box

The Prompt for Filename box in the upper left corner of the window shows which file commands prompt you to verify the intended file's name when the command is executed. Normally, the Edit File and View File commands require no prompt, but the Print File and Delete File commands do, as an added control feature.

For the purposes of this tutorial, toggle off the Delete File option now. There is another safeguard to make sure you don't accidentally erase a file, as we will see a little later. If you wish, you can turn this option back on at the end of the step.

The Tool Icons box

The Tool Icons box allows you to choose which of five Norton programs (SmartErase, Printers, Norton Backup, Viewer, and Shredder) you want to have active as a Desktop icon. If you select

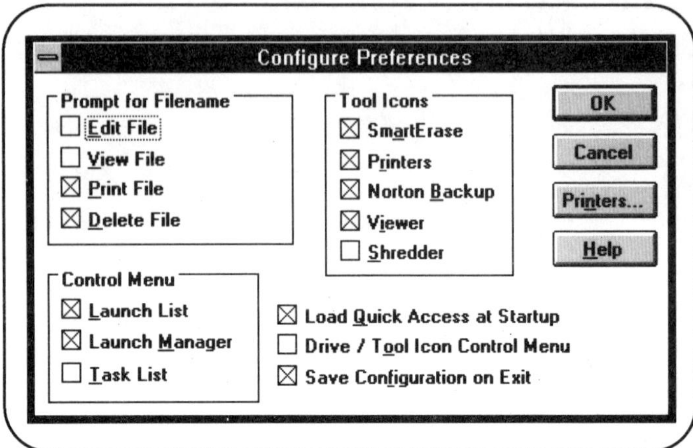

Figure 16.1: Configuring preferences

Printers, click the Printers button to the right of the Tool Icons box and select those printers you have installed that you want to appear on the Desktop.

Below the Tool Icons box are three general configuration options. The Load Quick Access at Startup option starts Quick Access when you start the Desktop and makes all groups available on the Window menu. The Save Configuration on Exit option saves the current state of the Desktop when you quit Windows, keeping its configuration constant from session to session. Both of these options are toggled on by default and should remain so. The Drive/Tool Icon Control Menu, toggled off by default, enables a control menu for the tool and drive icons found on screen. When this option is toggled on, you can click once on an icon to see this menu. Available options let you open the icon into a window, close or remove the icon from the screen, rename the icon, or change it altogether (tools only).

The Control Menu box

The options in the Control Menu box provide alternate methods of starting and switching programs via the control box of any running Windows program. The Launch List is a list of programs you can run. The Launch Manager allows you to edit the Launch List. These will be discussed in detail in Step 19. The Task List allows you to switch between programs currently running.

Configuring Confirmation

Many people consider it a standard of responsible program design to request that users confirm their intent to commit serious file operations (such as deleting a file or a directory). Confirmation requests prove valuable in preventing you from losing data when you are not paying attention. However, if you frequently delete files, or if you are deleting a long list of them, you may find it annoying to be asked whether you really want to delete each one.

You can turn off some of these safeguarding prompts by selecting the Confirmation option from the Configure menu on the Desktop. There are five file operations whose confirmation you can suppress:

- Delete: The standard file deletion procedure.
- Subtree Delete: Deletes an entire subdirectory.
- Replace: Overwrites one file with another.
- Mouse Operation: Allows you to perform a file operation by clicking and dragging icons with the mouse.
- Unformatted Print: Sends a file—in an unformatted state—directly to the printer if the Desktop is unable to print the file using the application the file was created with. Printing such files can result in garbage, hence the warning.

If confirmation is on, an X appears in the box to the left of the operation to indicate that it is selected. Norton is set up with all five operations requiring confirmation.

To show how this feature works, let's make a file and compare how the Delete operation functions with and without confirmation. To make a file:

1. Open the Notepad and type

   `This is yet another sample file.`

2. Save the file with the title C:\NDW\ERASEME.TXT and close the Notepad and its group window.

3. Now double-click on the C drive icon. Click on the \NDW directory and select the sample file.
4. Click on the Delete button. You will see a confirmation dialog window like the one shown in Figure 16.2.
5. Click on No so the file will not be deleted.

Now let's suppress the confirmation for deleting a file. To do so:

1. Select Confirmation from the Configure menu.
2. Toggle off the Delete option.
3. Click OK.

Now try deleting ERASEME.TXT. Notice that it doesn't ask you to confirm.

The Drive Icon Location and Display

When you launch the Norton Desktop, each of your drives appears as an icon in a column at the left side of your Desktop. You can configure the Desktop to suppress the display of the drive icons, to display only some of the drive icons, or to display the drive icons in another location on the Desktop. Of course, you can drag any of the drive icons to a more out-of-the-way location at any time using the mouse.

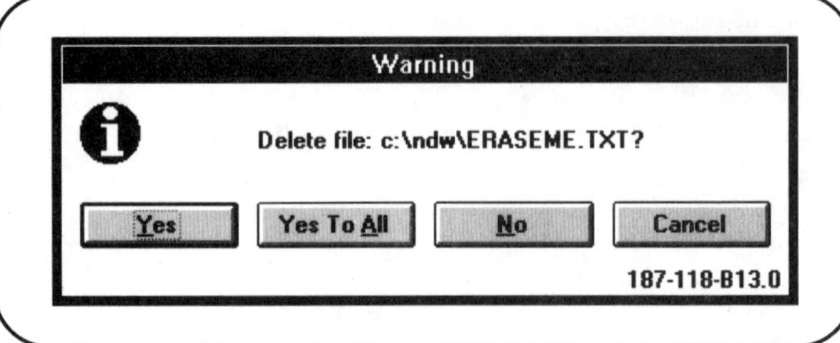

Figure 16.2: Delete with Confirmation on

Select Drive Icons from the Configure menu. You will see a window like that shown in Figure 16.3. The drives that will appear on the Desktop are displayed in the Drives box on the left side. Notice that by default all the drives are selected.

You can select or undo the selection of a single drive by clicking on its icon in the Drives box. Click each one of your drive icons now, so that none is selected. Click OK. The drive icons have disappeared from the Desktop.

Now select Drive Icons from the Configure menu again. To display only certain types of drives, click on the appropriate selection in the Drive Types box. For instance, to display only hard disk drives, click on the All Hard Drives option. This highlights the drive icons in the Drives box. Now click OK again. Only your hard disk drive icons will show up on the Desktop.

The Display Drive Icons option can also be used to turn the display on and off. To turn off the display of the drive icons without deselecting them, you can toggle off the Display Drive Icons option.

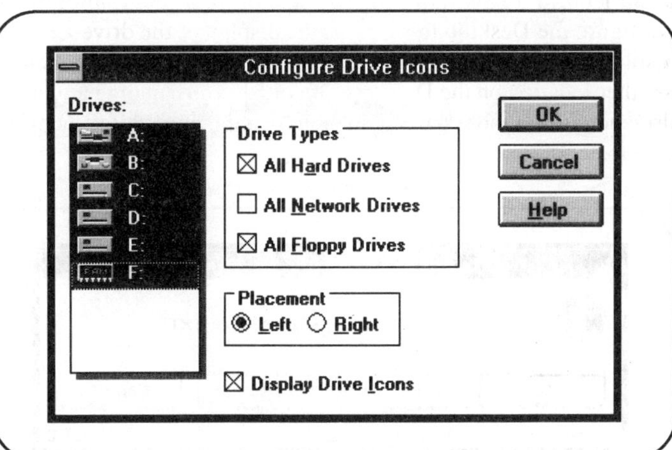

Figure 16.3: The Configure Drive Icons window

Select the Drive Icons option once more. Choose those drive icons you want to see on the Desktop. Now click on Right in the Placement box and click OK. The drive icons now appear on the right-hand side of the screen.

Changing the Buttons on the Drive Windows Button Bar

Each of the Norton Desktop's drive windows has six buttons arrayed across the bottom of its frame. Each button is assigned to one of the most common file operations of most users. These are Move, Copy, Delete, View Pane, SuperFind, and Select All. If you have a Desktop command you use more often and would like to assign it to one of these buttons, it is quite a simple process.

Let's say you rarely use the Move command, but you rename your files quite often. Follow these steps to replace the Move command on the button bar with the Rename command:

1. Select Button Bar from the Configure menu. You will see the window in Figure 16.4.

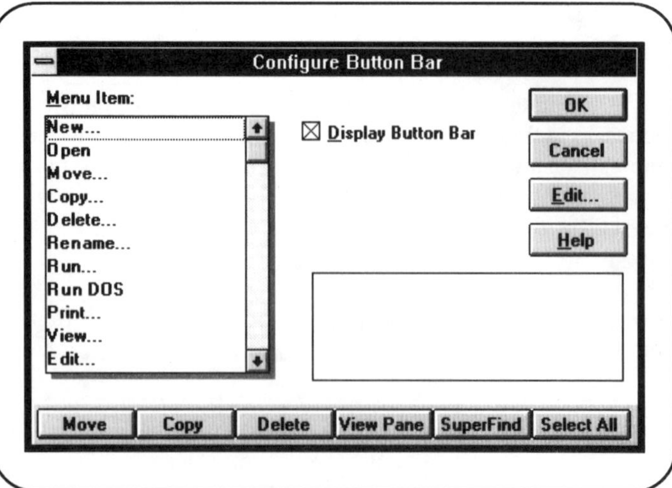

Figure 16.4: The Configure Button Bar window

2. Find the Rename command in the Menu Item box on the left side of the window. Click on Rename to select it.
3. Now click on the Move button at the bottom of the frame. The button changes to Rename.

Now let's change the button bar back to its original form.

1. Click on Move in the Menu Item box to select it.
2. Click on the Rename button. It changes to Move.
3. Now we have an ellipsis (three dots) after the word *Move*. Recall that before we began this exercise, the Move button did not have an ellipsis. To restore the Move button to its original state, click Edit. This brings up a window that allows you to edit the text of each button. (This is especially useful if you add a menu item with a lengthy name, such as Find Previous, that won't fit on the button.) The Move button is already highlighted.
4. Highlight just the three dots with your mouse and press Delete to delete the ellipsis.
5. Click OK twice to accept the changes to the button bar.

Assigning Shortcut Keys

Just as the button bar gives you a quicker way to accomplish common tasks in the drive window, you can use shortcut keys to further automate your work with the Norton Desktop menus. To assign new keys to menu options, or to reassign existing ones, select Shortcut Keys from the Configure menu. The Configure Shortcut Keys window appears.

Now let's assign a shortcut key combination for the Rename command.

1. Click on Rename in the Menu Item box. The New Key box displays the word *None,* indicating there's no shortcut key for this command.

2. Click on the box containing the word *None*.
3. Now we'll assign a key combination. You can use the Ctrl key or the Ctrl and Alt keys in combination with any letter, number, or direction key. You can also use function keys alone or with the Shift, Alt, and Ctrl keys in any combination (except for F1, reserved for Help). We will use Ctrl-N, to remind us of Re*N*ame. Press Ctrl-N now. The text "Ctrl+N" appears in the New Key box.
4. If you want to see the shortcut key displayed next to the menu option, click Include key name in standard menu.
5. To assign the key combination to this command, click OK.
6. To remove the key assignment for this command and revert to None, pull down the Configure menu and select Shortcut Keys. Select Rename on the menu item list, click once on the new key box, and press the Spacebar. Click OK to leave the window.

There are several things to take note of when assigning shortcut keys:

- Don't use keys you've already assigned to the Launch Manager. The Launch Manager will override the standard menu shortcut key assignments. The Launch Manager will be discussed in Step 19.
- These key assignments apply only to the standard menus, not custom menus (see Step 17 for more details on custom menus).
- The numbers on top of your keyboard are viewed as separate keys from those on the numeric pad. Thus you can assign Ctrl-1 (using the top row) and Ctrl-1 (using the numeric pad) as separate shortcut keys.

Step 17

Customizing Menus I

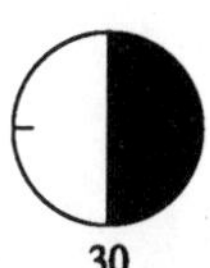

If the Norton Desktop's pull-down menus are not configured to your liking, you can easily customize them to better suit your needs. You can rearrange the items on the existing menus to the configuration you're the most comfortable with, or you can create completely new menus and add them to the menu bar.

In this step we will make changes to the existing Desktop menus and add a new menu. The tutorial should take you about 30 minutes to complete

Using Custom Menus

Sometimes in the course of your work you will find that you want to add a command to an existing menu. Let's say you want to put the Disk Doctor tool on the Disk menu so that all disk-related functions are together on the same menu. To add the Disk Doctor command to the Disk menu, follow these steps:

1. Select Edit Custom Menus from the Configure menu. You will see the Menu Assignments window shown in Figure 17.1.
2. Select Disk Doctor from the Commands box.
3. Scroll through the Menu box until you come to the Disk menu. Each indented entry represents a menu item. The dashed lines separate groups of items that belong together. Click on the dashed line immediately below Label Disk. (If Label Disk does not appear, click on whatever item immediately precedes the View menu.)
4. Click the Add button. The command Disk Doctor will appear directly below Label Disk, as shown in Figure 17.2.
5. Now click the Test button. A window with a sample menu bar will appear. Pull down the Disk menu; the Disk Doctor command will appear there.

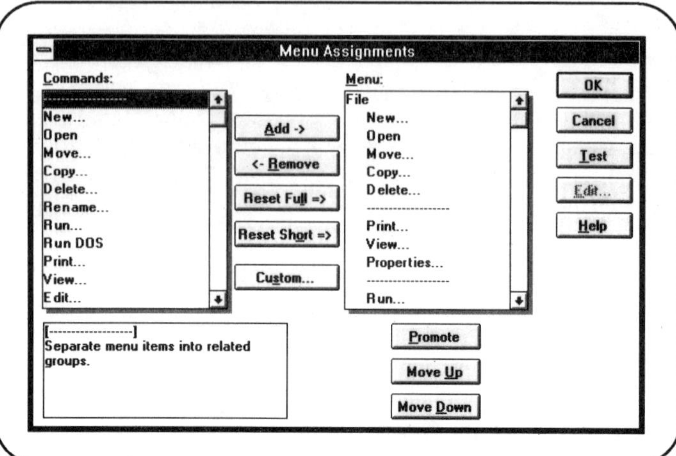

Figure 17.1: The Menu Assignments window

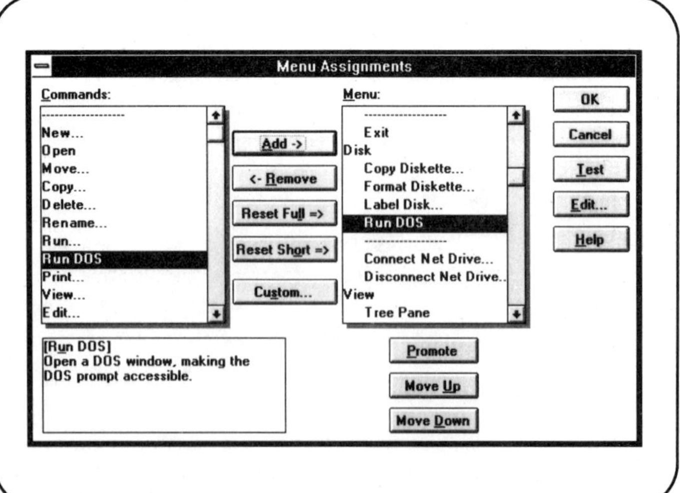

Figure 17.2: Adding a menu item

6. Close the Menu Test window and then click Reset Full and OK. The menus will revert to their standard format. Leave the Menu Assignments window open for now.

Adding Menus to the Desktop

You can also create entirely new menus to serve your own particular needs. Let's say you find yourself using your word processor more than anything else on your computer. Wouldn't it be convenient to have a menu that allows you to access your word processor directly from the menu bar? In this section, we'll create a menu called WP that serves this function. Then we'll add SuperFind and the Windows Notepad as menu items, so we can create, edit, and find text from a single menu.

1. Click the Custom button. The Create Customized Menu Item window will appear, as shown in Figure 17.3.
2. In the Type of item box, select New Menu.
3. Click inside the Text box and type **WP**, the name of the new menu.
4. Click OK. You will return to the Menu Assignments window, and the WP menu will appear at the top of the list.
5. Click Test.

Adding a shortcut key

Notice that the WP menu doesn't have an underlined letter for keyboard access. We can change this menu to include such a key.

1. Close the Menu Test window.
2. With WP still selected, click Edit.
3. Place the cursor in front of the letter *P* in the word *WP* in the Text box. Type an ampersand (&), and click OK. The letter following the ampersand will become the keyboard access key.

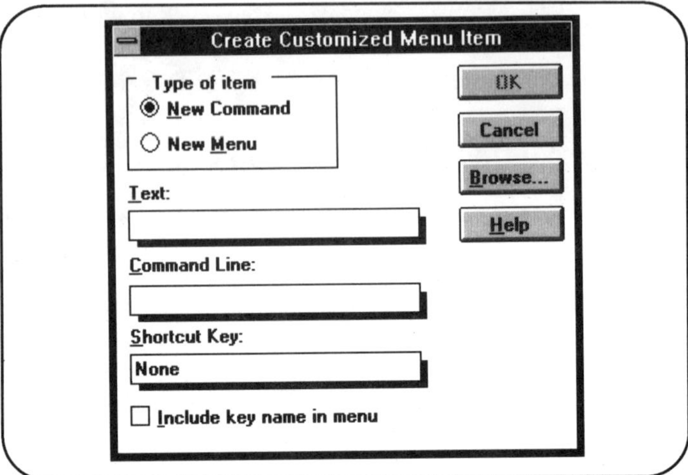

Figure 17.3: Creating a customized menu item

4. Click Test again. The WP menu will display an underscore beneath the *P*. You can now reach the menu by pressing Alt-P when you are using the custom menus.
5. Close the Menu Test menu.

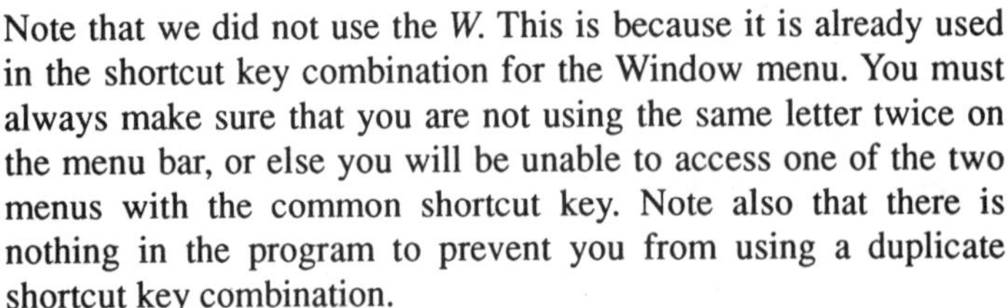

Note that we did not use the *W*. This is because it is already used in the shortcut key combination for the Window menu. You must always make sure that you are not using the same letter twice on the menu bar, or else you will be unable to access one of the two menus with the common shortcut key. Note also that there is nothing in the program to prevent you from using a duplicate shortcut key combination.

Adding Desktop Commands to a Custom Menu

A new menu is not very useful without any commands on it! Let's add some items to the WP menu.

1. Select the dashed line below the WP menu in the Menu box.

2. You will be reminded that you can't have an empty menu. Click OK.
3. Select SuperFind from the Commands box and click the Add button.
4. Click Test and pull down the Sample menu. You will see that the menu now has a menu item: SuperFind.
5. Close the Menu Test menu.

Adding DOS and Windows Commands to a Custom Menu

You are by no means limited to the commands already provided somewhere else on the Norton Desktop's menu bar. Almost any DOS or Windows executable file (that is, a file with the file extension .EXE or .COM) can be added as a menu item. We will add the Windows Notepad as a custom command to the sample WP menu. (You can substitute your own word processor here if you wish.)

1. Select the dashed line that's now directly below the SuperFind item in the Menu box.
2. Click the Custom button.
3. In the Type of item box, select New Command.
4. In the Text box, type **Notepad**. This is the command that will appear on the menu.
5. Click once in the Command Line box. Here you must enter the full name and path of the command you are adding.
6. Click the Browse button. Scroll through the directories in the Tree box until you have located the WINDOWS directory and click once on it.
7. Scroll through the Files box and click once on NOTEPAD.EXE.
8. Click OK. At this point you could assign a shortcut key for the menu option (see "Assigning Shortcut Keys" in Step 16 for more information). Click OK once more.

9. Click Test again to see the WP menu with two menu items: SuperFind and Notepad, as shown in Figure 17.4. Close the Menu Test window.
10. Click OK to see the WP menu on your menu bar.

Now your WP menu is a normal, functioning Desktop menu. To test it, pull down the WP menu and select the Notepad. Close the Notepad again.

This brings us to the end of the step. We will explore menu customization further in Step 18.

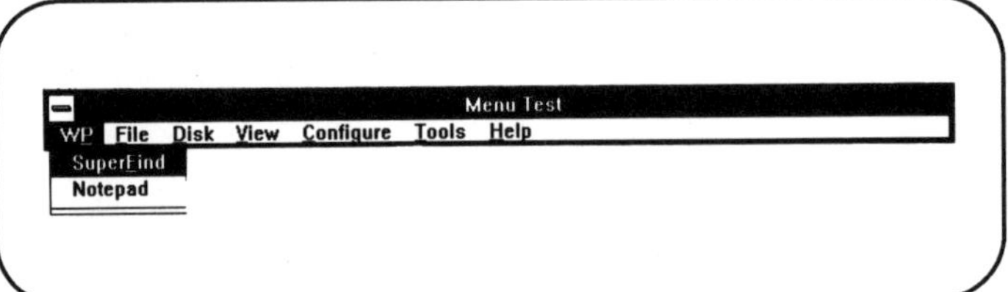

Figure 17.4: The WP menu

Step 18

Customizing Menus II

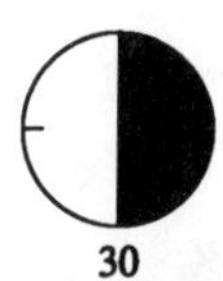

Step 17 introduced you to customizing menus. This step continues with this topic and covers the rearrangement of menus and menu items, the creation of submenus, turning custom menus on and off, and deleting them altogether.

Rearranging Menus and Menu Items

We have seen how you can create new menus and add to existing ones. Menus and menu items can also be moved around quite easily and the menus' hierarchy can be changed readily as well. To do this, we'll use the Promote, Move Up, and Move Down commands.

1. Pull down the Configure menu and select Edit Custom Menus. This brings up the Menu Assignments window again.
2. Select the Notepad item of the WP menu (which you created in Step 17) in the Menu box.
3. Select Exit from the Commands box.
4. Click Add. The new menu item, Exit, now comes between SuperFind and Notepad, but it would seem most appropriate at the end. Let's move it there now.
5. Click Move Down twice: once to move Exit below Notepad, and once to move it below the dashed line.
6. Now click Test and pull down the Sample menu to see the effect.
7. Close the Menu Test window.

Now let's say you want the Exit command to be the easiest to get at of all the commands. You could take out a step in its execution by making it a menu by itself on the menu bar. That way, you would simply click the Exit menu to leave the Desktop.

1. To make the Exit menu item to a menu, click on Exit, if it is not already highlighted, and then click on Promote.
2. Click Test again to see the effect, and then close the Menu Test window.
3. Now get rid of the Exit menu by highlighting and clicking Remove.

Creating Submenus

You can also create submenus for the Norton Desktop. While pulling down a submenu does add another step to executing a command, submenus can be useful for condensing menus that have become too long. We will give an example here.

1. To clear things up, remove the dashed line below Notepad by selecting the line and clicking Remove.
2. Click Custom and choose New Menu for the Type of item.
3. Click once in the Text box, type **&Modify Text,** and click OK. Notice how the new menu automatically goes to the top of the list.
4. With the new Modify Text menu selected, click the Move Down button twice. It should appear just below SuperFind, indented the same distance.
5. Select Notepad and click Move Up. As you can see from the indentation, the Notepad menu item has now become an item on the Modify Text submenu.
6. Select the indented dashed line below Notepad and then select Edit in the Commands box.
7. Click Add. The Edit and Notepad commands are now both items on the Modify Text submenu.
8. Click Test and pull down the WP menu to see the effect; a rightward-pointing arrow after the Modify Text item indicates that it contains a submenu.
9. Click on Modify Text; you should see a submenu pop up to the right of the WP menu, as shown in Figure 18.1.

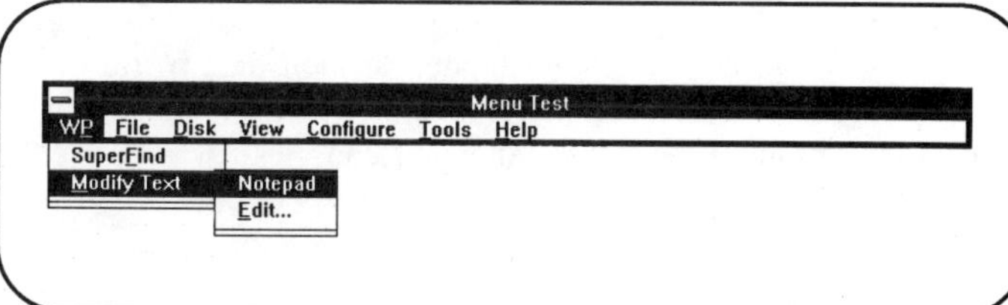

Figure 18.1: A submenu

10. Close the Menu Test window and save your work so far by clicking OK.

Turning Custom Menus On and Off

When you add a custom menu to the Desktop, it appears at the far left of the Norton Desktop menu bar, as our WP menu does now. You can change the horizontal order of the menus by using the Promote, Move Up, and Move Down commands as you did with individual menu items. You can switch back to the standard menu display by selecting Standard Menus from the Configure menu. Select Custom Menus from the Configure menu to bring back your custom menus.

Deleting All Custom Menus

This brings you to the end of the tutorial. To remove the sample menus and menu option we created, you could use the Remove option, discussed earlier. This, however, would be inefficient as you would have to remove items one at a time. To delete *all* of your custom menus in one fell swoop, do the following:

1. Pull down the Configure menu and select Edit Custom Menus.

2. On the Menu Assignments dialog window, select the Reset Full option.
3. Click OK to confirm the removal of custom menus.

The Reset Full option sets only full menus back to their original state. If you had added custom menus to the Short menu group, these would not be affected. To remove all custom menus from the Short menu group, select Reset Short instead.

Step 19

The Launch List

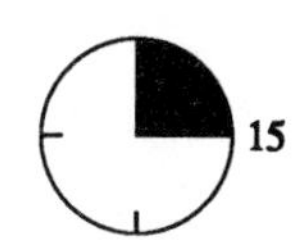

We have seen how placing program icons on the Desktop makes the launching of applications easier. There may be times, however, when you want to have an uncluttered Desktop. Or perhaps you prefer accessing software from a pull-down menu. The Norton Launch List was designed to this end. It allows you to launch an application right from the Control menu, just by selecting a menu item. This step contains a brief tour of the Launch List. It should take you about 15 minutes to complete.

Accessing the Launch List

To access the Launch List, click once on the Norton Desktop control box at the upper left corner of the screen, just above the File menu. The Launch List is also available from the Control menu of any running Windows program or minimized icon.

You will see a menu like one you would normally see with the Program Manager, except that there are two additional options: Launch Manager and Launch List. Select Launch List and you will see a list of programs, as in Figure 19.1. To start any of these programs, simply select the menu option you want.

Adding to the Launch List

You will probably find that there are programs that you use more frequently than the default selections on the Launch List. To add a program of your choosing, do the following:

1. Pull down the Control menu and select Launch Manager. The window shown in Figure 19.2 will appear.
2. Now click the Add button. The Add Launch List Item window will appear.
3. In the Text box, type the name of the program you wish to add. For the example here, type **Notepad**.

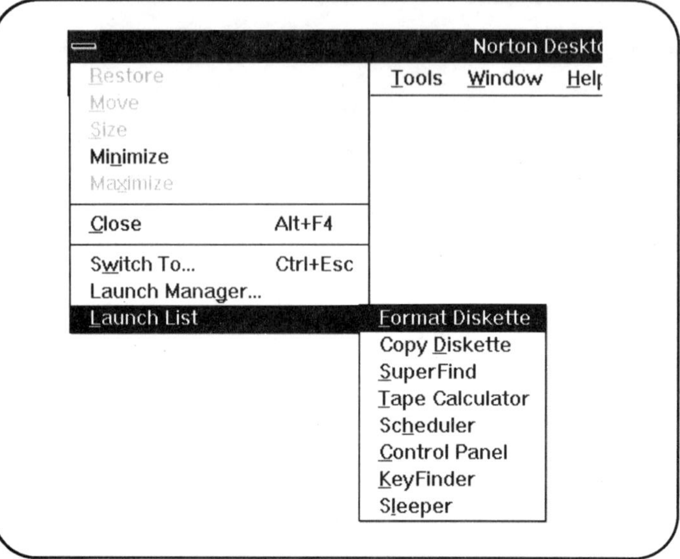

Figure 19.1: The Launch List

4. Click on the Command Line box and enter the name of the program file, complete with path. Type

   `c:\windows\notepad.exe`

   and click OK.

5. The word *Notepad* appears at the bottom of the Menu Items box. Click OK.

Launching a Program

You have now made it possible to load the Notepad from the Launch List. Try doing so now: Click on the Desktop's Control menu. Select Launch List to see the "tear-off" menu again. Select Notepad, and the Notepad window will appear. Now close it again.

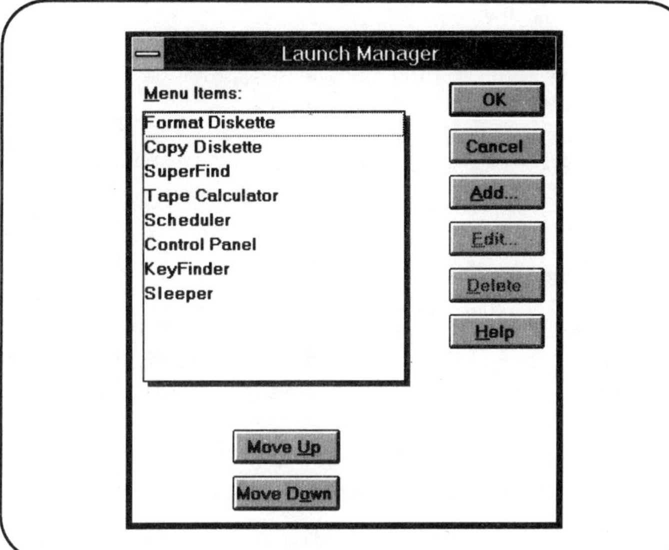

Figure 19.2: The Launch Manager

Adding Shortcut Keys to the Launch List

You may have noticed that the Launch List has a shortcut key option. Let's go back and add a shortcut key for the Notepad.

1. Pull down the Control menu and select Launch Manager.
2. Highlight the Notepad option and click Edit.
3. Click once in the Shortcut Key box and press your shortcut key. For this example, use Ctrl-N.

Valid shortcut key combinations are the Ctrl key or the Ctrl + Alt keys and any letter number or direction key. Function keys can also be used alone (except F1, reserved for Help) or together with the Ctrl, Alt, and Shift keys in any combination.

4. Toggle on the Include key name in menu option. This will cause the shortcut key to appear next to the program name on the Launch List.

5. Click OK twice.

Pull down the Control menu again and select Launch List to see your work. Ctrl-N appears next to Notepad.

These shortcut key assignments take precedence over other shortcut keys and are active in Windows applications as well.

Changing the Launch List Order

Items in the Launch List appear in the order in which they were added; the most recent addition appears at the bottom. But you can order the list in any way you choose. Let's move Notepad to the top.

1. Select Launch Manager again from the Control menu.
2. On the Launch Manager window, select Notepad.
3. Click Move Up until Notepad moves to the top of the list.
4. Now click Move Down to move Notepad down a bit.
5. When you have positioned it where you want it, click OK. The next time you see the Launch List, its options will be reordered.

Deleting Items from the Launch List

To remove an item from the Launch List, do the following:

1. Select the Launch Manager from the Control menu.
2. Select the item you want to remove (Notepad) and click Delete. Note that you can only delete items one at a time.
3. Click OK to remove Notepad from the Launch List.

Step 20

The Batch Builder

Batch files are text files that automatically execute commands in sequence. For example, you could create a batch file that would execute—in one action—the commands to clear the screen, to change a directory, and to run the program you want. Thus you can use batch files to perform repetitive tasks and further automate your work.

With the Norton Desktop Batch Builder, you can devise elaborate batch files using over 100 commands in its Windows batch language. In this step, you will create two simple batch files and add one batch file to a custom menu. The tutorial should take you about 45 minutes to complete.

The Batch Builder Window

The Batch Builder is accessible from the Tools menu when Full Menus are enabled. If you have been using Short Menus, select Full Menus from the Configure menu to reset the menu bar. Then select Batch Builder from the Tools menu.

The Batch Builder menus

You will notice that the Batch Builder window has a menu bar much like that of the Notepad, with File, Edit, Search, and Help menus. These menus are essentially stripped-down versions of the Notepad menus, containing commands for editing the batch programs you create with the Batch Builder. The Reference menu, located between the Search and Help menus, is a handy online reference to all the batch commands at your disposal. Select it now. The Reference window appears.

To the left, the Commands box displays the entire list of available batch commands. Scroll through the list to get an idea what kinds of commands are available. Click on one of the commands as you scroll through the list. The Description box will display information on this command, followed by the command's syntax and an example using the command.

Command syntax

The *syntax* is the set of rules governing how command lines are structured. The command syntax may demand that commands are followed by *parameters* enclosed in parentheses. Parameters are pieces of information, such as file names or a text string you want displayed, that some commands require you to supply. If a parameter is a text string, it must be enclosed in quotes. If there are several parameters, they are separated by commas.

Batch programming commands can be confusing if you are not familiar with programming languages. Because of space limitations, we cannot discuss the more advanced commands in the Desktop's Windows batch language in this book; for this, consult your Batch Builder manuals. However, if you don't fully understand batch programming, don't worry. We can create a few batch files whose command structure is nearly self-evident.

Creating Windows Batch Files

Let's start by creating a sample program that beeps and displays a short message.

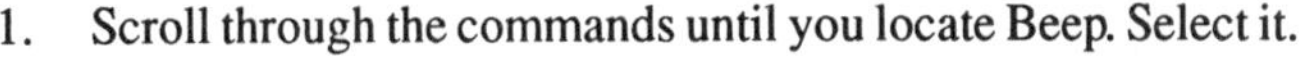

1. Scroll through the commands until you locate Beep. Select it.
2. Now look again at the Description box. It gives you a description of the command's function, followed by its proper syntax and an example. With this command, everything is quite straightforward.
3. Click Add. The Beep command is inserted at the cursor in the Batch Builder window.
4. Press Enter. This ensures that the next command we place in the batch file appears on the line below the Beep command.

You don't have to select the commands from the Reference menu; you can type them in if you prefer.

5. Click the Reference window to make it active.
6. Scroll through the list and select Message. Read the information in the Description box.

7. Make sure that the cursor in the Batch Builder window is on the line following the Beep command, and click Add to insert the Message command into the batch file.
8. After and on the same line as *Message,* type

   ```
   ("First Batch File","Hello, world!")
   ```

9. Now select Save As from the File menu, name the file FIRST.WBT, and click OK.
10. Close the Batch Builder window.

Running a batch file

You have now created your first Batch Builder program. It is located in the NDW directory. To run the program, select Run from the Desktop's File menu (not the Batch Builder File menu) and then type

```
c:\ndw\first.wbt
```

in the Command Line box. Then click OK. You will hear a beep and see a window with the title "First Batch File." The message "Hello, world!" will be displayed, as shown in Figure 20.1. Click OK to exit the batch file.

Of course, the whole idea of writing batch programs is to further automate your computer activity and make your use of Windows more efficient. If you write a batch file that performs a specific task that you find useful and do rather often, you should place the batch file's icon onto the Desktop by dragging it from the opened drive

Figure 20.1: The "Hello, world!" batch file

window. Or you can add it to the Launch List as discussed in the previous step, or add it as a menu item on a customized menu.

Incorporating Batch Programs into the Menu System

Now we will create a batch program, called "Free Space on Drive C," that reports the amount of free space left on drive C. We will then add it to the Disk menu using the Edit Custom Menus command.

1. Select Batch Builder from the Tools menu.
2. Select Reference.
3. Scroll through the commands list on the Reference window and select DiskFree. Review the command's description, syntax, and the example.
4. Click in the Batch Builder window and type

   ```
   size =
   ```

5. Click Add in the Reference window. The DiskFree command appears after *size* =.
6. Complete the command by adding the drive parameter. Type

   ```
   ("c")
   ```

   The first line should now read

   ```
   size = DiskFree("c")
   ```

7. Press Enter to start a new line.
8. Click in the Commands box of the Reference window and scroll down to select Message.
9. Now click Add to insert the Message command into the second line of the batch program.

10. Type in the remaining text so that the line appears as follows:

    ```
    Message("Total bytes free on drive C:",
    size)
    ```

    Note that the first parameter, the window's title, is a text string and therefore in quotes. The second parameter, *size,* is a variable defined in the first line of the program and requires no quotes.

11. Now save the file with the name C:\NDW\DISKFREE.WBT.

Adding a batch program to a menu

Since this batch program checks drive C for free space, it's only logical to add it to the custom Disk menu. To do so:

1. Close the Batch Builder.
2. Select Edit Custom Menus from the Configure menu.
3. Place the cursor on the Format Diskette command in the Menu box.
4. Click Custom.
5. For Type of item, select New Command.
6. In the Text box, type

    ```
    Free Space on Drive C
    ```

7. In the Command Line box, type

    ```
    c:\ndw\diskfree.wbt
    ```

    and click OK.
8. The new item appears in the Disk menu in the Menu box. Click Move Down to place it just below Format Diskette.
9. Click Test and view the menu item as it will appear on the custom menu bar by pulling down the Disk menu. Then close the Test window.
10. Click OK.

From now on, when you pull down the Disk menu and select Free Space on Drive C, the number of bytes free will appear in a window labeled "Total bytes free on drive C:" If you want to remove this batch file from the Disk menu, select the Edit Custom Menus option on the Configure menu, highlight Free Space on Drive C, and click Remove.

Index

D

E

F

G

H

I

U

V

W